C000220871

DELI

Its Monuments and History

T. G. P. SPEAR

Updated and Annotated by
NARAYANI GUPTA
and
LAURA SYKES

Illustrations by Ripin Kalra

DELHI
OXFORD UNIVERSITY PRESS
CALCUTTA CHENNAI MUMBAI
1997

Oxford University Press, Great Clarendon Street, Oxford OX2 6DP

Oxford   New York
Athens   Auckland   Bangkok   Calcutta
Cape Town   Chennai   Dar es Salaam   Delhi
Florence   Hong Kong   Istanbul   Karachi
Kuala Lumpur   Madrid   Melbourne   Mexico City
Mumbai   Nairobi   Paris   Singapore
Taipei   Tokyo   Toronto

and associates in

Berlin   Ibadan

© Oxford University Press 1994
First published 1943
Second edition 1945
Reissued with annotations 1994
Oxford India Paperbacks 1997

ISBN 0 19 563923 5

Typeset by Rastrixi, New Delhi 110 070
Printed in India at Pauls Press, New Delhi 110 020
and published by Manzar Khan, Oxford University Press
YMCA Library Building, Jai Singh Road, New Delhi 110 001

CONTENTS

vi   *Contents*

Percival Spear
1901 – 1982

FOREWORD

Narayani Gupta

The city of Delhi is as full of surprises as a good treasure-hunt. You may suddenly find a ruined arch many hundred years old beside a recently-built bungalow, or see the reflection of a highrise building in the waters of an ancient step-well. We all have to discover Delhi for ourselves. It is possible to spend many happy winter afternoons wandering, wondering, imagining . . . but before venturing out, it is pleasant to have someone tell you where to go, and what to look for. Percival Spear's book was written 50 years ago, and you will soon see that it is different from other 'guidebooks'. Spear *speaks* to us. He was an Englishman who taught history at St. Stephen's College, Delhi. He himself became interested in Indian history and is today known as the author of Volume 2 of the Penguin *History of India*. He also enjoyed learning the history of Delhi, on which he wrote three books. One of them was *Delhi — Its Monuments and History*, which was printed in two editions (1943 and 1945) and was used as a textbook for schools. Copies of this book are not easy to find, and we have prepared this annotated 3rd edition because we think that no other book has quite replaced it. Spear's writing is full of his love for the place and a sense of respect for the individuals who have made the city—architects, rulers, poets, pious men. These qualities are missing in more sophisticated guidebooks. As he talks to readers, he leads them through the city, on foot, on bicycle, and even by car along the long stretches of Lutyens' New Delhi.

Though Spear would have been happy to have visitors to Delhi use his book, I think he was writing essentially for the *children* of the city. In those days, there was no TV and little cinema to make claims on children's leisure hours, school homework was sensibly limited, and the town was small, with a few trams and only one bus-service. Places like Sultan Ghari and Masjid Moth lay in the middle of fields far out of the city. To visit the Qutb or Hauz Khas meant leisurely rides by *tonga*, and the time there was spent in pleasant picnics un-disturbed by canned music from players or transistors, and interrupted only by the rising crescendo of the brainfever bird or the shriek of homing parakeets. The pace was slow, and allowed visitors not just to 'see' monuments but to spend some time there absorbing the ambience . . .

Spear would be as bewildered by today's Delhi as the two old village women of Munirka who said sadly 'Ever since the tarred roads were laid out, we can never find our way from Mehrauli to Munirka'. The town of 7 lakh people Spear knew now holds a restless 93 lakhs. Most of them have come to the city recently, and are so busy trying to survive or push ahead that they have not had time to look at Delhi. As the population grows, many of the smaller monuments 'disappear' or get hidden behind housing blocks. Very few of the inhabitants of Panchsheel Park have visited the neighbouring Begumpuri Masjid, which figures as a major monument of the Islamic World (Michell, p. 268). The landscape that Spear knew – the rugged hills of the Ridge, the river, the streams and fields, also 'disappear' under new 'colonies'. The tiny blue boards of the Archaeological Survey of India (ASI) are obscured by gigantic hoardings and by road signs. It is easy to see the signboards for the National Zoological Park (the 'Zoo' to most of us) but difficult to find the nearby Humayun's tomb, the stupendous architectural marvel which is known as the precursor of the Taj Mahal. The colours and the polish of the buildings have been worn off by time and vandalism, and stones and pillars have been stolen. Many of Spear's students, Hindu and Muslim, could read Persian, and many monuments were a literary as well as artistic delight. Today few people can decipher the inscriptions.

All this makes it more important than ever before that we should know and care for our monuments. Delhi is frequently compared to Rome – and this is understandable, because both cities have an *embarras de richesses* as far as historic architecture goes. Between sunrise and sunset, there is *so much* to be seen *for free* (with only a nominal entrance fee at the Lal Qila, Humayun's Tomb and Safdarjang's Tomb).

When we visit the monuments, we are treading the footsteps of visitors over centuries.

On Tuesday I visited the mausoleum of Nizamuddin Auliya. . . . The same night I circumambulated the tomb of Khwaja Kutbuddin, and visited the tombs and palaces of Sultan Ghiyasuddin Balban, of Sultan Alauddin Khilji, and his minaret, the Hauz Shamsi, the Hauz Khas, the tombs and gardens of Sultan Bahlol and Sultan Sikander Lodi.

This was a diary entry of a visitor in 1526 (obviously the monuments were not closed at sunset in those days!). His name was Zahiruddin Mohammad, popularly called 'Babur' (Tiger). Babur was referring to three centuries of Sultanate architecture, to which his own dynasty was to add many more monuments. Later, the British, always fascinated by the charisma of Delhi, built a capital meant to last 500 years.

There is no obvious way to organize a book on Delhi's monuments. It could be done geographically, moving from south to north (the average Delhi tour 'does' 'New Delhi' in the morning and 'Old Delhi' in the afternoon). It could be in historical order, which means one will zigzag from place to place. Spear's is a third pattern – he starts with the area which would have been most familiar to the children, who then all lived in what is called 'Old Delhi' (i.e. north of Delhi Gate). For him, as a student of the fortunes of the Mughal dynasty, the Lal Qila of Shahjahan was the obvious central reference point. Starting from the Qila and Shahjahanabad, he moves to the Civil Lines, where the homes of several Europeans were located, and the University of Delhi. He then conducts the students south to Firoz Shah Kotla, and still further to Purana Qila, Humayun's tomb and Nizamuddin. Later they take bicycle rides out to Sayyid and Lodi Delhi, and to Safdarjang's tomb. Whole day excursions are organized to the still further Qutb complex, and Suraj Kund. Then there is a motorcar drive through New Delhi after a fascinatingly long session at Jantar Mantar.

The endpaper at the beginning of this book is reproduced from Spear's book, and gives us an idea of what Delhi looked like in 1943. The endpaper at the back fills in the main roads subsequently built. Delhi has become so built up that many of the routes he describes are no longer in use. Because of his informal style of writing, some of the buildings he describes could not be identified with certainty. It is also possible that some may have been demolished in the last fifty years. We hope that this edition, annotated and also illustrated with lively sketches by a gifted young artist and student of architecture, will induce citizens and students of Delhi to follow in Spear's footprints and bicycle tracks!

This book is teeming with people. Bringing history to life by imaginative interaction with monuments can be done so easily in Delhi. Until the 1960s students of class 10 had to answer a compulsory question on the monuments of Delhi. In Delhi University, for the compulsory English language paper, there was a frequently repeated question asking students to narrate 'a conversation between Old and New Delhi'. Spear's little book, and Hindi and Urdu books called *Hamari Dilli* were read as textbooks.

One of the interesting things about Spear's style is the throwaway fashion in which he refers to incidents of history or to 'famous' people. He was steeped in history and assumed the students were likewise. They probably were: in those days when curricula were less burdensome, interaction between teachers and students was closer, and the reading habit more ingrained. Present-day readers will greatly benefit by reading Spear's *Twilight of the Mughals*, which describes Delhi in the eighteenth and nineteenth centuries. In the present edition, the Chronological Chart is our attempt to situate in time the people and the buildings he describes. Likewise, Spear was familiar enough with Urdu and Persian terms, but for present-day readers who might not be, we have appended a Glossary.

Spear occasionally refers the reader to other books. In our notes, we have also cited books and authors, in abbreviated form. The full titles and other details will be found in our Bibliography. In the small city of Delhi which Spear knew, it was possible to indicate which books could be found in which libraries with a sense of certitude. The number of libraries in Delhi has grown, but the older books are difficult to locate, unless they have been reprinted. Our annotated bibliography will indicate which of the books he refers to are available. It also suggests others which should be of interest. We have also compiled an Index for easy reference and cross-reference.

We have thoroughly enjoyed working on this, and hope it will draw lots of Delhiwalas out into the wonderful history with which they are surrounded.

ACKNOWLEDGEMENTS

Many people have encouraged us, helped us with information or made suggestions. If anyone's name has been inadvertently left out, we apologize.

Mona Aggarwal, Ravi Dayal, A.K. Damodaran, Premola Ghosh, Niharika Gupta, Parthasarathi Gupta, Nigel Hankin, Jagbir Singh and Jaipal Singh, Jyotindra Jain, Nishaat Manzar, Indira Menon, Ratish Nanda, Ramji Narayanan, Nirupama Raghavan, R.V. Smith, Nita Srinivasan, Robert Sykes, Father Ian Weathrall, the staff of the British Council Division, the staff of the India International Centre Library, and of course the Conservation Society, Delhi.

HOW TO READ THIS BOOK

T. G. P. Spear
(1943)

This book is not meant to be read all at once, like a novel. Nor is it meant to be learnt by heart, like a textbook. But I do want you to read it, and this is the way you should do so.

You should read this book a chapter at a time. When you have a lesson on the Tughlaqs, read the chapter on Tughlaqabad. When reading about Firoz Shah, read the chapter on Firoz Shah Kotla and Hauz Khas. When you read about Humayun and Sher Shah look up the chapter on the Purana Kila; when Shah Jehan is the subject, look up the chapter on the Fort. When you have done this, try to go and see the places you have read about. You need not wait for your teacher to organize parties. If you have a bicycle you can go to many places in an afternoon with your friends.

Another way to read the book is this. Whenever you visit a monument – with your friends, your family or your school-fellows – read, on your return, the chapter about it in the book. When, for instance, you go to the Qutb or the Lodi Park, look up the book afterwards and see what it says about them. Read the chapter on architecture in little bits. When you visit Hindu buildings, see what it says about Hindu architecture, and when you visit a Mogul monument, see what it says about the Mogul style, and so on.

The book is not meant to worry you but to help you to understand history and to enjoy the great and beautiful monuments which lie all around you in Delhi.

In St Paul's Cathedral, London, there is a tablet to the architect, Sir Christopher Wren. Underneath it there is an inscription in Latin which says, 'If you seek his monument, look around you'. Similarly, if you seek the monuments of history in Delhi, look around you.

FOREWORD TO SECOND EDITION

T. G. P. Spear
(1945)

This book was originally written for the school boys and girls of Delhi, by whom it is now being used. Its purpose was to help them discover for themselves the glories of their city, that knowing it more fully they would value it more truly. For this reason it was written as simply as possible and the matter is divided into ordinary chapters with additional notes for more interested or advanced students. This must be the plea if the style seems too simple or references to teachers irritating. On the principle that seeing is believing, directions are given for reaching the more distant places. The chapters are divided geographically; separate monuments or groups of buildings near each other are dealt with in turn. At the end is a short chapter on Delhi architecture.

When the book was written before the war, it was not even intended to publish it in English. But since then Delhi has received hundreds of guests, more or less permanent, more or less willing, and a need has been felt for some book which would describe the principal monuments and give some of their historical background. War-time preoccupations forbid the writing of any fresh book, so the existing one has been slightly adapted and provided with illustrations and a sketch map in the hope of doing something to meet this need. If this edition helps to kindle the imagination of any visitor with the magic of imperial centuries, it will have been worth while. In this hope it is offered by a lover of Delhi to her guests of war and peace.

LAL QILA

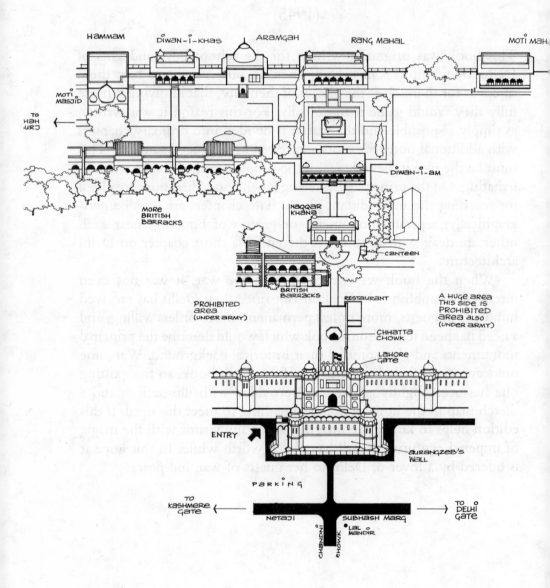

HAMMAM   DIWAN-I-KHAS   ARAMGAH   RANG MAHAL   MOTI MAH

MOTI MASJID

TO HAH HURJ

MORE BRITISH BARRACKS

DIWAN-I-AM

NAQQAR KHANA

CANTEEN

BRITISH BARRACKS

PROHIBITED AREA (UNDER ARMY)

A HUGE AREA THIS SIDE IS PROHIBITED AREA ALSO (UNDER ARMY)

RESTAURANT

CHHATTA CHOWK

LAHORE GATE

ENTRY

AURANGZEB'S WALL

PARKING

TO KASHMERE GATE ←   NETAJI   SUBHASH MARG   → TO DELHI GATE

CHANDNI CHOWK

LAL MANDIR

N

Part I

THE CITY

1. THE FORT

We will start our study of Delhi by visiting the most famous non-religious monument of the city, the palace of Shahjahan. The people have always called it the Lal Qila or Red Fort. But Shahjahan called it the *Urdu-i-Mu'alla*. In the time of Akbar Shah II and Bahadur Shah it was called the *Qila-i-Mu'alla* or the Fort of Exalted Dignity.

Shahjahan's is the most famous of all Indian royal palaces. It is a model of all the others. First let us understand the different parts of a royal palace. Every palace had at its entrance a *Naqqar Khana* or *Naubat Khana*. There the imperial band played several times a day, and the great royal drums were kept. None but royalty might use them. Next comes the Hall of Public Audience or *Diwan-i-Am*. This is where the emperor sat in public Durbar. He received ambassadors, reviewed troops, and transacted public business. Then comes the *Diwan-i-Khas* or Hall of Private Audience. Here the emperor received private visitors and his counsellors of state. Admission to the Diwan-i-Khas was a great privilege like membership of the Cabinet today.[1] Beside this the emperor had his private rooms where he entertained his friends. A Mughal palace always had some magnificent baths or *hammam*, and a mosque for the emperor's private prayers. Then there was the zenana. There was always in the zenana a special palace which belonged to the Padshah Begum,[2] or chief lady of the Court.

The first thing to notice in Shahjahan's palace is the great wall or curtain which stands in front of the Lahore Gate. This was built by Aurangzeb, and its object was to save the nobles the trouble of walking the whole length of the Chandni Chowk. Everyone had to walk in

---

[1] At the time Spear was writing, Indian children would have been familiar with the Cabinet system, both in Britain and, since 1937, in Indian provinces. The Cabinet was introduced in the Central Government in 1947, after Independence.

[2] The Padshah Begum, or 'First Lady', was usually of royal blood, not just the current favourite concubine.

the presence of the emperor. Before this wall was built the emperor, when he sat in the Diwan-i-Am, could see right down the Chowk.[1]

Inside the Lahore Gate[2] is the *Chhatta Chowk*, or covered bazaar. This covered bazaar is unique in Mughal architecture. Here the merchants of Delhi sold their goods to the nobles of the Court.

Passing though the Chhatta Chowk we come to the *Naqqar Khana*. Here the imperial band played six times a day. The musicians sat upstairs, where there is now a war museum. This was the entrance to the palace proper. The Emperor Ahmad Shah was murdered in this building in 1754. Between the Naqqar Khana and the Fort wall was a space occupied by the quarters of the troops on guard at the palace gates. It was a great privilege to guard the palace and was much sought after. The Rajputs were often on duty.

Inside the Naqqar Khana is the *Diwan-i-Am*. The hedges mark the positions of the old walls. The Diwan-i-Am was covered with white plaster or *chunam*. Within the pavilion the nobles stood in rows facing each other according to their rank. The royal princes stood next to the throne, and the *Wazir* sat on the marble *takht* below it. The emperor sat above and you can see the door by which he entered. Shahjahan and Aurangzeb sat here twice a day on most days of the week. The lesser nobles stood outside the Hall. There was a special

---

[1] Shahjahan must have had extraordinary eyesight! Court etiquette decreed that, so long as the nobles were in view of the emperor, they were obliged to move about only on foot, not on horseback or in palanquins, and to bow constantly as they walked as a mark of respect for the emperor. Aurangzeb probably found all this protocol as irksome as his courtiers and had the considerate idea of building a wall which blocked the view of the Qila from the rest of the city of Shahjahanabad. Thus, at a single stroke, the courtiers in Chandni Chowk simply became invisible to Aurangzeb and were free to come and go as they pleased.

'Chandni Chowk' actually referred to the octagonal 'chowk' (open space) outside the Begum Bagh. It contained a central pool which reflected 'chandni' (moonlight). (It is sometimes said that the Chowk was named after its silversmiths, but this is a confusion of the word 'chandi', meaning silver, with 'chandni'). It has since come to include the whole, originally un-named, street built in 1650 by Shahjahan's daughter, Jahanara Begum. This leads from the Lahore (i.e. western) Gate of the Lal Qila to the Fatehpuri Masjid.

[2] Lahore Gate is the Lal Qila's main (western) gate; the southern gate is called Delhi Gate. These should not be confused with the Lahore and Delhi *city* gates (see p. 11 note 2).

railing to separate them from the rest of the crowd. Behind the emperor's throne there is some mosaic work done by a French artist.[1] The Mughals were proud of their foreign artists and employed as many as possible. One of the pictures is of a man playing a violin. This represents Orpheus, the Greek god of music. These stones were taken away at the Mutiny (1857), but Lord Curzon discovered them in London and put them back here. In the hot weather great red curtains were hung round the Hall to keep off the sun. You can still see the rings to which they were fixed.

To the left of the Diwan-i-Am is a path which leads out of the court. Here was a gateway called the *Lal Purdah*, because a red curtain hung there. It was a great privilege to enter this gate. Only the emperor's special favourites did so. They were called *Lal Purdaris*.

Next we come to the *Diwan-i-Khas*. The throne in the Hall is the one which took the place of the Peacock Throne which Nadir Shah carried away to Persia.[2] Here Nadir Shah sat when he gave the empire back to Mohammed Shah. It was much used by the late emperors. Here Ghulam Qadir[3] blinded Shah Alam, and here Shah Alam received Lord Lake, the British General, in 1803.[4] King George V held a Durbar here in 1911 and the Prince of Wales another in 1921.

Turn left and you come to the royal baths. Close to these is the mosque or private royal chapel.[5] On state occasions the emperor went to the Jama Masjid, but otherwise he prayed in this mosque. Aurang-

[1] The artist was *not* French: 'While the *pietra dura* decoration in the Agra *jharoka* appears to be solely the work of Mughal artists, the indigenous work of the Delhi *jharoka* is combined with imported Italian material' (Koch, *Shahjahan and Orpheus*, p.16).

[2] In 1739 the Persian Emperor, Nadir Shah, defeated the army of the Mughal Emperor, Mohammed Shah, at Karnal. When the people of Delhi rose against him, he exacted retribution by unleashing a massacre of the population. He carried away booty to the estimated value of 700 million rupees including the Peacock Throne and the Koh-i-Noor diamond (Swamy and Ravi, p. 171).

[3] Ghulam Qadir was 'a Rohilla chieftain who seized Delhi and blinded Shah Alam in 1787 in a fit of frenzied frustration at his failure to find expected treasure in the palace' (Spear, *Oxford History of India*, p. 487).

[4] In 1803, Lord Lake defeated the Marathas who controlled Delhi, thus gaining control of the plain between the Ganga and the Yamuna, as well as the provinces of Delhi and Agra. Under the subsequent treaty, Shah Alam, 'who had been left by the Marathas as a puppet, recognised British authority in exchange for protection and maintenance' (Spear, *A Historical Sketch*, p. 77).

[5] The Moti Masjid (Pearl Mosque).

zeb built this mosque and often prayed here. Now we enter the palace
garden. It is a fine example of a Mughal garden and was called the
Hayat Baksh garden. Part of it is covered by the barracks.[1] Beyond
this garden was another called the Moonlight Garden or Mehtab Bagh
because it contained flowers which blossomed by moonlight.

You can see where the water ran down stone waterfalls. At the
end of the terrace is the *Shah Burj*,[2] where the emperor held secret
meetings with his ministers. From this tower Prince Jehandar Bakht,
eldest son of Shah Alam, was let down by a rope when he fled from
Delhi in 1787. The little pavilion half-way along the terrace was built
by Akbar Shah II. He and Bahadur Shah often sat there. The
flower-beds show the course of the stream which ran right through
the palace. It was called the *Nahar-i-Behisht* or Stream of Paradise,
and it was fed by an aqueduct from the canal which ran through the
Chandni Chowk.

Now we will return to the Diwan-i-Khas. On the other side of
the Hall are the private apartments of the emperor. One of these is
furnished in Mughal style and you should look at it very carefully.
Notice the scales of justice carved in the marble of the *Baithak* (sitting
room). Here the emperor entertained his friends. The *jharoka* or
balcony is the place where the emperors sat to show themselves to
the crowds. The people gathered on the plain below and the emperors
sat there once a day.

Beyond the private apartments is the *Rang Mahal* or Palace of
Colour. This was the palace of the Padshah Begum. It was much
damaged in the eighteenth and nineteenth centuries. But it was once
very beautiful indeed. Beyond this is another building which is now
the museum.[3] It is full of interesting things which your teachers will
explain to you. Notice specially the Mughal costumes and the pictures. You must come here many times before you can see everything. The rest of the zenana was pulled down to make room for the
barracks.[4]

[1] These were built after the Revolt of 1857, when the British army occupied the
Fort.

[2] *Shah Burj* means Royal Pavilion.

[3] The museum is housed in Mumtaz (Exalted) Mahal (Hall).

[4] Many of the buildings inside the Lal Qila were 'cleared' by the British army after
the Revolt of 1857, *who* then built their barracks there. Nearly half a century later,
Lord Curzon did what he could to preserve the beauty of the remaining structures.

ADDITIONAL NOTES[1]

The Archaeological Department has published an excellent guide to the palace (price Re 1). It has a picture of the palace as it used to be. You should study this carefully and it will tell you all you want to know about the palace. There is a separate guide and catalogue to the Museum. This you should also have (so that you can explain it to your pupils). The following points may be mentioned:

(i) The swivel guns in the verandahs. These were placed on camels. Nadir Shah used them with great effect at the battle of Karnal.[2]

(ii) The Mughal paintings inside the museum.

(iii) The Mughal costumes, including dresses of Zinat Mahal Begum and Bahadur Shah,[3] taken after the Mutiny.

(iv) The various ornaments (chessmen, etc) in the glass cases.

The Mughal ceremonial is described by the Frenchman Bernier in his *Travels*. Lane Poole in his *Mediaeval India* quotes from him.

Notice as you walk round how the different parts of the Palace fit together. Then read the inscription in the Diwan-i-Khas.[4]

You may wonder why the Mughals built their halls with only pillars but no walls. The reason is that they came from central Asia where they always lived in tents. The kings held their Durbars in great tents or shamianas. When the Mughals came to India and were rich they built in stone, but they still thought of their tents. The Diwan-i-Am is a shamiana in stone.

A branch of the Jumna used to flow between Salimgarh[5] and the Fort. It then joined the main river which ran roughly where the modern road now is. There was thus a space where crowds could gather and animal-fights (of which the Mughals were very fond) could take place.

---

[1] See pp. 106–9 for more on the architecture of Shahjahanabad.

[2] There are no longer any swivel guns (*zamburak*) on the verandahs.

[3] Bahadur Shah II was the last Mughal Emperor and Zinat Mahal was his wife.

[4] Inscribed on the corner arches of the northern and southern walls is the couplet attributed to Shahjahan's minister, Saadullah:

'*Agar firdaus bar ru-i-zamin ast, Hamin ast, hamin ast, o hamin ast*'

(If on earth there be a place of bliss, it is this, it is this, O it is this!)

The same quotation is used in the Shalimar Gardens in Srinagar (see Crowe and Haywood, p. 102).

[5] See p. 15 for more on Salimgarh, which was under army control from 1857 to 1991, but is now 'protected' by the Archaeological Survey of India (ASI).

2. THE MOSQUES OF DELHI

The best and biggest mosque of India is the **Jama Masjid**[1] of Delhi.
There are very few mosques in the world that are bigger. You can
yourself go and see this mosque. When you enter the mosque stand
in this courtyard and look at its beautiful proportions, its shapely
domes and the Arabic inscriptions against a background of white
marble. Then climb up one of the minarets and look at the view
around you.[2] You will notice that the mosque is situated on a rock
and that there is no place higher than this in the city.[3] The Red Fort
also is lower. A great emperor like Shahjahan chose the highest and
best site for this house of worship.

The Jama Masjid was built by Shahjahan. The architect was Ustad
Khalil. You should respect the architect as much as the emperor,
because such architects are not born very frequently in this world. If
either the architect or the emperor had not existed we should not
have possessed such a magnificent building. The greatest quality of
this building is that from whatever point or in whatever light you
look at it, it still retains its beauty. Whether it is sunrise or sunset,
night or day, moonlight or broad daylight, its charm is always the
same. Looked at from any angle its grandeur remains the same.
Whenever you pass by look at it carefully, and you will yourself
recognise the truth of this statement. The present imam is the
descendant of the imam appointed by Shahjahan himself; thus there
is a link with the Mughal period in Delhi even now. The Jama Masjid
is the best of all Mughal mosques, therefore you should study its
characteristics closely.[4] Two of the special features of Mughal mosques
are their domes and their minarets. Before the time of the Mughals

[1] See glossary for a note on the confusion between Jama Masjid (congregational
mosque) and 'Juma' Masjid ('Friday' mosque). *Jamna* Masjid was also 'a common
corruption' (*Hobson-Jobson*).

[2] Visitors are still allowed to climb the minaret in the southern corner of the
courtyard on payment of Rs 5, so long as the time for prayers is not imminent and
there is at least one man in the party.

[3] There are now obviously higher buildings in Delhi, but the mosque still dominates
Shahjahanabad, as the emperor intended. It is enormously large: the courtyard is 100
metres square.

[4] See pp. 108–9 for more on the architecture of the Jama Masjid.

separate minarets were not added to mosques in Delhi. A mosque with minarets which are detached from the main building in Delhi is always one built in the Mughal period. The other special feature is their domes.[1] The early sultans only built *half-domes* – that is a dome which is a quarter circle only. The Mughals introduced *full* domes. These are domes which are a full semicircle. You can see this kind of dome in Humayun's Tomb. But then the Mughals went further. They made the domes more than a semicircle so that it curved inwards at the bottom, like this. The band at the bottom before the dome starts is called the *drum* (be-cause it is shaped like one). This form of dome is called bulbous,

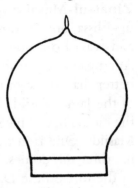

FIG. 1

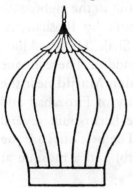

FIG. 2

because it looks something like a bulb. The Mughals used marble for their domes whenever they could. But they added little strips of black marble in the white like this. You can see them in the Jama Masjid and in the other Mughal mosques of Delhi. After the Jama Masjid, the most important mosque in Delhi is the *Fatehpuri Masjid* at the end of the Chandni Chowk. It was built by Fatehpuri Begum, a wife of Shahjahan. The materials and work of the mosque are very good but the whole building is not as fine as the Jama Masjid. The reason for this is that the proportions of the building are not so good. In particular the domes do not seem to fit the mosque as well as they do on the Jama Masjid. When the parts of a building fit together so that the whole building looks beautiful, we say that the building is well proportioned. When they do not fit together we say that the building is not well proportioned. Sometimes the different parts are each of them good but the whole effect is not pleasing. This is what has happened to the Fatehpuri Masjid. Like the Jama Masjid, it still has a lot of property and endow- ments. Some of this is used to help poor students.[2]

[1] See pp. 105 and 107 for more on the architecture of domes and tombs.

[2] Mosques were usually financially endowed by their original patrons, under the system of *Waqf*, covering both the physical maintenance of the building and its

There is a fine mosque in Daryaganj which many people know very little about. But it is one of the largest in Delhi. It is called the **Zinat-ul-Masajid** (Ornament of Mosques).[1] It was built by Zinat-un-Nissa, one of Aurangzeb's daughters. She was a very pious woman and was also a good Persian poet. She was the Padshah Begum of Aurangzeb's court for some time. The proportions of the mosque are better than those of the Fatehpuri, but they are not so good as those of the Jama Masjid. There is one more mosque of special interest in the city. That is the **Sonehri Masjid**.[2] There are in fact two Sonehri Masjids. One is in the Chandni Chowk, close to the **Kotwali**,[3] and has three gilt domes. The other stands by itself on the maidan in front of the fort on the Daryaganj side. This one is very small and has no gilt on its domes. It was on the roof of the mosque by the Kotwali that Nadir Shah sat when he ordered the massacre of Delhi citizens on 22 March 1739. These mosques were both built in the eighteenth century. That in the Chandni Chowk was built by Roshan-ad-Daulah, the favourite Minister of Mohammed Shah. He was killed at the battle of Karnal and is buried at Nizamuddin. There is one more mosque which you must visit. It is the **Kalan Masjid** near the Turkoman Gate. It is a relic of Firoz Shah's city of Firozabad and was built by his *Wazir,* Khan-e-Jahan. Khan-e-Jahan built several mosques, and all of them are very much alike.[4] The best ones are the Kalan Masjid, the Khirki Masjid (near the Qutb) and a mosque at

charitable activities. The Archaeological Survey of India supplements the Waqf Board in the case of 'protected' buildings.

[1] Zinat-ul Masajid means 'the most beautiful of mosques'. It was also called the Ghata Masjid (Cloud Mosque) because it was white with black stripes.

[2] Sonehri Masjid means 'Golden Mosque'. The gilt is still intact.

[3] The Mughal Kotwali (police station) is now part of the Sisganj Gurdwara (Sikh temple) compound.

[4] Junan Shah Telingani, Khan-e-Jahan, is said to have built seven mosques in Delhi, five of which survive: the Kalan Masjids (Big Mosque) at Nizamuddin and Shahjahanabad, the Khirki Masjid, the Begumpuri Masjid and Kalu Serai Masjid. The Khirki Masjid ('Window Mosque') is on the Qutb–Saket road, in the centre of Khirki village. It is called this because of its distinctive window openings, filled in with *jali* tracery. Junan Shah Telingani, from Telingana in present-day Andhra Pradesh, was the son of Maqbul Khan Telingani. Both he and his father before him served as prime minister to Firoz Shah Tughlaq, hence the Khan-e-Jahan title. (This was not particularly unusual: until 1947, many Indian princely states also had hereditary prime ministers.)

Nizamuddin. The Kalan Masjid is a typical example of a Tughlaq mosque, and like all Tughlaq buildings, it has very little ornament. But its proportions are very good indeed.

ADDITIONAL NOTES

The special points of the Mughal style are dealt with in the section on architecture.[1] There is one thing which is useful to remember. It is that the later the date of a mosque the more bulbous is the shape of its dome. Also, the later the date, the larger are the black strips on the dome. Compare the thin stripes of the Jama Masjid with those of the Zinat-ul-Masajid, which was built fifty years later. Later mosques have thicker stripes still. The later mosques also do not have such good workmanship. This is a rough guide to the dates of Mughal mosques. You can visit the Mughal mosques in connection with your lessons on the Mughal emperors. You can read any inscriptions they contain, and find out when they were built and who built them. Then Kalan Masjid can be visited when you are reading about Firoz Shah.

3. THE CITY

The city of Delhi is full of every kind of historical monument. There are mosques, palaces, houses, serais, streets and gardens. Some of the greatest and most exciting events in India have happened here. You can walk all over the city for yourself, and here we shall only mention some of the more important places.

Shahjahan's streets. Shahjahan built three great streets in Shahjahanabad. He did this so that there might be sufficient space for the great state processions. The streets of Agra were very narrow and this was one of the reasons why Shahjahan came to Delhi. These three great streets were the Chandni Chowk, a road from the Delhi Gate of the Fort to the Jama Masjid, and a road from the Delhi Gate of the Fort to the Delhi Gate of the city. Part of this road is now the Faiz Bazaar.[2] The road to the Jama Masjid and its bazaar was destroyed

---

[1] Chapter 22 below.

[2] The street from the Akbarabadi (i.e. southern) Gate of the Lal Qila to the city gate of the same name (Akbarabad = Mughal Agra). Later these Gates became known

after the Mutiny when all the houses on the present maidan were taken away. This road was used by the emperors when they went in state to the Jama Masjid. The Chandni Chowk was the chief road for processions. Here Shahjahan and Aurangzeb passed in pomp; here Dara Shikoh was led a prisoner through the sorrowful Delhi crowds; here Nadir Shah and Ahmad Shah Abdali rode in triumph. Here came Madhav Rao Sindhia, the Maratha, and Ghulam Qadir, the Rohilla. The last state procession was in 1912 when Lord Hardinge entered Delhi, for the first time.[1] The Chandni Chowk is one of the most historic streets in the world. In Mughal times a canal ran down the centre. This was restored in 1829 when Ali Mardan's canal was repaired.[2] But about 1910 it was covered in and now runs under-ground. The present Queen's Gardens once contained the royal serai for travellers and it was then known as the Begum Serai.[3]

The walls. The walls were built by Shahjahan and repaired by the British. A walk round them is very interesting. The distance is about four and a half miles.

Where the wall has been taken away a road follows the line of the wall. The towers which you find at intervals are called bastions. The big square ones were added by the British. The stretches of wall in between are called 'curtains'. Cannons were placed in the bastions which could shoot anyone trying to climb the curtains. The bastions were said to command the curtain walls. At intervals you will find round towers detached from the walls. They were also built by the British. They are called Martello towers after an engineer called

as the *Delhi* Gates, and the street as Faiz Bazaar (Bazaar of Plenty). After Independence, the street was renamed Subhas Chandra Bose Marg after the 'Netaji' (leader) of the 1940s Indian National Army (INA).

[1] Lord Hardinge, as Viceroy, of course participated in the Delhi Coronation Durbar of 1911–12, at which King George V announced the transfer of the capital from Calcutta to Delhi. Spear is here referring to Hardinge's own ceremonial 'state entry' into Delhi which took place a year later, in the winter of 1912.

[2] Ali Mardan Khan was a Persian who joined the service of Shahjahan in 1637, and rose to the rank of Amir-ul-Umara. He was involved in many of Shahjahan's ambitious building plans (see p. 24).

[3] The Begum Serai and surrounding Begum Bagh were named after their founder, Jahanara Begum. After 1857, the serai's walls 'disappeared'; one pavilion survives. The Town Hall and Hardinge (now Hardayal) Public Library were built on the site, and Begum Bagh was renamed Queen's Gardens by the British in honour of Queen Victoria. What remains of the garden is now called Mahatma Gandhi Park.

Martello, who invented them.[1] Their purpose was the same as the bastions. You can tell the parts of the wall built by Shahjahan and the parts built by the British by the stones they used. Shahjahan used a thin red brick, the British square blocks of Delhi stone. As you go round count up the gates and make a list of them. Then see which ones have now been taken away.[2] All the fighting in the Mutiny took place on the north side from the Kashmir to the Lahore Gates. When the Marathas attacked Delhi in 1804 the fighting was on the south side, from the Delhi to the Ajmer Gate.

The Anglo-Arabic College. This is the only Mughal **madarsa** which is still a place of education. It was founded by the father of the first Nizam,[3] Ghaziuddin Khan, who died in 1710, and himself lies buried there. It has been in turn an Arabic madarsa, an oriental college, a police station, a high school, and it is now a college again.[4] The plan of the college is a model for other colleges in India, with its mosque and beautiful courtyard.

The grave of Sultan Raziya. Sultan Raziya was the only empress of India in Muslim times.[5] She reigned from 1236–40 and was then deposed by the nobles. Her grave is near the Turkoman Gate, in Muhulla Bulbuli Khan.

Nineteenth-century buildings. Though the buildings of the nineteenth century are not of great value from the artistic point of

[1] Nigel Hankin has written that the name is derived from Cape Martella in Corsica; the design was copied by the British after 1805.

[2] The term 'walled city' is used for Shahjahanabad, but much of the wall has been demolished since 1857, to provide outlets for the railway lines and roads. The original 14 *city* gates (as opposed to the gates of the Lal Qila itself) were, going anti-clockwise: Kashmir, Mori, Kabul, Lahore, Farash Khana, Ajmer, Turkman, Delhi, and (by the river) Khairati, Raj Ghat, Calcutta, Nigambodh, Kela and Badar Rao. The only ones still standing are: Ajmeri, Delhi, Kashmir and Turkman; an arch has replaced the gate at Nigambodh. There is a stretch of wall running south to east from Delhi Gate, which it is possible to walk along.

[3] The only princes to bear the title of 'Nizam' were the rulers of Hyderabad.

[4] Spear is referring to Delhi College, later called Zakir Husain College. This has moved to new premises nearby, and the building is once again occupied by the Anglo-Arabic High School (see p. 15, note 3).

[5] Sultan Raziya would have objected to the title 'empress', lest it be thought she was a mere consort, and was rightly proud to have been chosen by her father Iltutmish as his successor in preference to her elder brother. By 'Muslim times', Spear means twelfth–nineteenth century (see Barton and Malone, *10 Easy Walks in Old Delhi*, pp. 48–9, for more on how to find her grave).

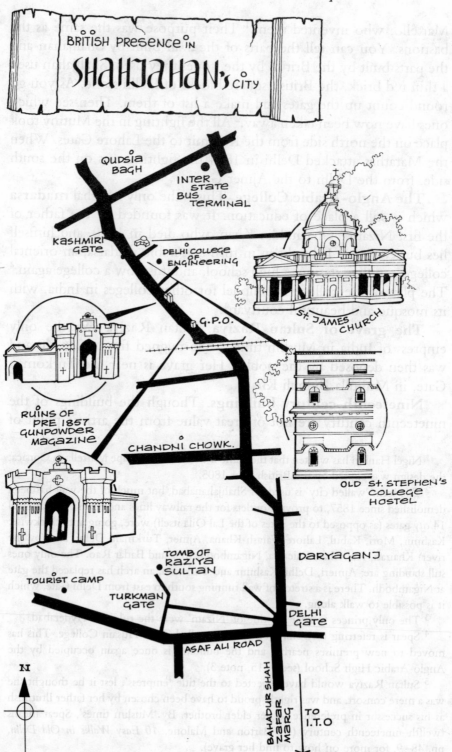

BRITISH PRESENCE IN
SHAHJAHAN's CITY

QUDSIA BAGH

INTER STATE BUS TERMINAL

KASHMIRI GATE

DELHI COLLEGE OF ENGINEERING

St. JAMES CHURCH

G.P.O.

RUINS OF PRE 1857 GUNPOWDER MAGAZINE

CHANDNI CHOWK.

OLD St. STEPHEN'S COLLEGE HOSTEL

TOMB OF RAZIYA SULTAN

DARYAGANJ

TOURIST CAMP

TURKMAN GATE

DELHI GATE

ASAF ALI ROAD

BAHADUR SHAH ZAFAR MARG

TO I.T.O

N

view, they have historical associations and we should not despise them. They serve to remind us of famous characters in the immediate past.

First let us visit Lloyd's Bank off the Chandni Chowk. You turn down a lane close to the Imperial Bank and you will see it in front of you. It was the Delhi palace of the Begum Samru of Sardhana. It was built a hundred and twenty years ago and is designed in the classical or Greek style which the British brought with them to India. The hall of the Bank is the old Durbar Hall.[1]

Next we will go to Kashmir Gate. As soon as you pass under the Lothian Bridge[2] you see some old buildings. The inscription tells you that this was the gateway of the magazine which was blown up in the Mutiny. Then we come to the Government High School. This was the first palace of Dara Shikoh.[3] Its grounds extended right to Kashmir Gate. In 1803 it became the British Residency. Lord Metcalfe and Sir David Ochterlony lived there. Bishop Heber, the famous traveller, stayed there. The British added the pillars and verandah which you now see.[4] A little further on you come to St James Church. This was built by the famous Colonel James Skinner. He first served Daulat Rao Sindhia. But when Sindhia was going to fight the British he was dismissed. He joined the British and raised a regiment known as Skinner's Horse. Once when he was in Sindhia's army he was left wounded on the battlefield. He vowed that if he escaped he would build a church to the glory of God. This is the church which he built. It was said to be an imitation of St Paul's Cathedral in London

[1] The Imperial Bank is now the State Bank of India and Lloyd's is the Central Bank, near which is the electrical goods market, Bhagirath Palace, named after the man who bought the Palace of Begum Samru. On her death in 1836 her extensive properties were the subject of a lengthy lawsuit, one of the many ways in which the novels of Charles Dickens (in this case *Bleak House*) recall nineteenth-century India (see Banerji).

[2] Lothian Bridge may have been named after Lt. Col. Lothian Kerr Scott (1841–1919), a kinsman of the Marquess of Lothian who was Under Secretary for India in 1931–32. He is known to have served with the Royal Engineers in India between 1862 and 1869 and the Delhi bridge was completed in 1867. The bridge was considerably rebuilt in the 1980s, to allow more traffic lanes.

[3] This gentle and scholarly son of Shahjahan was killed by his brother Aurangzeb in 1659.

[4] Now the office of the Archaeological Survey (ASI)'s Delhi Department and the campus of the Delhi College of Engineering; see also Additional Notes (p. 15).

but is actually modelled on a church in Venice.[1] Skinner is buried in the Church and his friend, William Fraser who was murdered in 1835, is buried in the compound.[2] You will see a Ball and a Cross in the compound.[3] This is the one which the mutineers shot at during the Mutiny.

Opposite the church stands the Hindu College. This was Colonel Skinner's Delhi house. His son lived on there until the Mutiny. It is a good example of the kind of houses which people built before the Mutiny all over north India. You will notice a small mosque just opposite the church. Some people say that Skinner built this mosque. This is wrong. There is an inscription in Persian which you can read for yourself. It was built by Fakruddin Khan in 1717.[4]

ADDITIONAL NOTES

There are many old houses in the city which once belonged to famous men. It will be interesting to inquire about these and find out if there are any in the neighbourhood of your school or home. Many houses between the Chandni Chowk and the Fort were swept away after the Mutiny, and many more were destroyed when the railway was built. Just outside the city are the **Roshanara Gardens** which the Princess Roshanara built and where she lies buried. They are well worth a visit, but remember that the

---

[1] The specific church in Venice is not known, but it is an amalgam of several Italian Baroque cruciform churches, perhaps closest to the Basilica di Superga at Turin, built by Filippo Juvarra, (1717–31).

[2] The tombstone of this Resident of Delhi during 1830–35 is on the west side of the churchyard and reads: 'Sacred to the memory of William Fraser Esq, late Commissioner and Agent to the Lt. Governor at Delhi and a local Major in Skinner's Horse. Cruelly murdered by an assassin 23 March 1835.' Thomas Metcalfe succeeded Fraser as Agent, as the post of Resident was called after 1832.

[3] During 1857 the original ball and cross which surmounted the dome were damaged during the fighting. Replicas were substituted on the dome during later restoration, the originals being cemented into a marble plinth in the churchyard, but these were stolen in the 1950s.

[4] No; the inscription states that Fakhrul Masajid was built by Fakhre Jahan (Pride of the World) Begum in 1728, in memory of her husband, Shujaat Khan. Incidentally, note Spear's assumption that the average guidebook reader could decipher Persian.

garden is not now arranged as Roshanara planned it. It is larger than it used to be and is arranged according to the English style[1] instead of the Mughal.

The Begum Samru's palace. A very pleasant trip in the cold weather is to Sardhana, which is twelve miles from Meerut. You can go there by bus. The Begum built two palaces there and a large church. It contains a very fine marble monument to the Begum, which was carved by an Italian artist.

Sadar Bazaar Road. The road which runs from the Sadar Bazaar to the Lady Reading Health School was built by Sir Charles Trevelyan. It was part of his plan for a model suburb of Delhi in 1830.[2] Trevelyan married the great Macaulay's sister and was the grandfather of Professor G.M. Trevelyan, the Regius Professor of History in Cambridge and the author of the best history of England which has yet been written.

The Government High School. This was the Residency before the Mutiny. Then it was used by the Delhi College, which was very famous in its day. After it closed St Stephen's College was opened to take its place and for a long time it was the only college in Delhi.[3] There is very little now left of Dara Shikoh's building, but in some of the classrooms you can see traces of Mughal carving.

Salimgarh. Salimgarh was built by Salim Shah Suri, the son of Sher Shah. Its purpose was to guard the ford of the Jumna. There is nothing now left of it except the walls. In Mughal times it was used as a state prison.. Dara Shikoh and others were confined there. Where the bridge now is there used to be a Bridge of Boats.[4]

[1] The gardens are park-like, with trees and walks in the English manner, rather than formally and geometrically laid out in the Mughal style. Parts of the Mughal buildings have been restored.

[2] He named his suburb 'Trevelyanganj' (see Gupta, *Delhi Between Two Empires*, map on p. xv, and p. 17). It is no longer distinguishable as a separate entity from the surrounding area.

[3] The *madarsa* was founded in 1692 by Mir Shihabuddin Ghaziuddin Imadulmulk of Bukhara. It was constituted as the Anglo-Arabic School/Delhi College in 1824. (It is an Islamic tradition to co-locate all places of learning, from primary to tertiary education.) In 1877 the government closed down the college, but the school continued to function. The college re-opened in the 1920s, was renamed after Zakir Husain in the 1970s.. It moved in the 1980s, but the school is still there.

[4] 'The Bridge of Boats connected the Salimgarh fortress with the opposite bank of the river, "many hundred yards in width". It was through this bridge that most of the supplies for the mutineers crossed over to the city' (Griffith, *A Narrative of the Siege at Delhi, 1857*). According to Hearn's *Delhi* (p. 142), 'The Bridge of Boats used to be opposite the Rajghat Gate until the Grand Trunk Road bridge was built in 1852, after which it was brought up to about the line of the railway bridge.' The tradition of

4. THE CIVIL LINES

There are many more historical monuments to the south of Delhi than to the north. But in the Civil Lines there are some very interesting ones, both British and pre-British.

Before the Mughal period, the Ridge was a place for hunting, as we shall see when we go there. Under the Mughals all this area was covered with gardens. The gardens and pavilions of the Mughals lined the river right up to Wazirabad. Behind the Ridge they extended near the canal right to Azadpur. All this area was the west end, both of Mughal and of British Delhi.

We will leave the city by the Kashmir Gate and first walk to the **Qudsia Gardens**.[1] Part of this is the old Qudsia Bagh built by Qudsia Begum, the wife of Mohammed Shah and the mother of Ahmad Shah. She was a great Mughal lady of the first half of the eighteenth century. You can still see the entrance gateway, the mosque and the two pavilions. They are now the Garden Superintendent's house and the Masonic Hall respectively.[2] There was once a fine stone terrace, which is now a green bank. The river ran just below along the Bela road.[3] There were many other gardens like this along the river and you can still see the old stones and bricks lying about.

Next we will go to the **Ridge**. The first thing to see is a small pillar near the Hindu Rao Hospital. This is part of an Asoka pillar and was set up here by Firoz Shah. He brought it from Meerut, where he found it, because he liked old monuments. There is another Asoka Column at Firoz Shah Kotla, which is complete. These pillars were

---

building a bridge of boats near Salimgarh from the end of one year's monsoon until the beginning of the next continued until 1991, since when the custom appears to have died out, possibly because the number of bridges now in use means that it is no longer needed.

[1] The once extensive Qudsia Gardens is now largely occupied by the Interstate Bus Terminal and tourist camp site, but the gateway, mosque and pavilions are still standing in attractively maintained gardens.

[2] The Garden Superintendent's house is now signposted 'House of Horticulture Director'; the Masonic Hall is now Jamuna Hall, a primary school and dispensary. There is a new Masonic Lodge building.

[3] The Bela road is now called Mahatma Gandhi Marg (Ring Road).

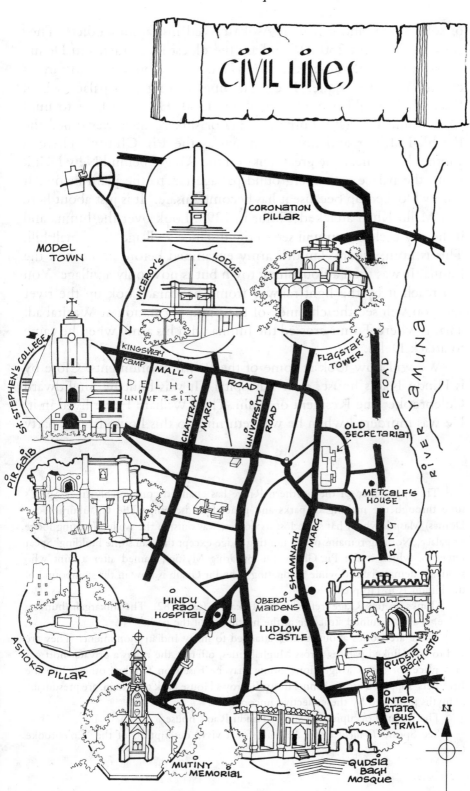

CIVIL LINES

MODEL TOWN

CORONATION PILLAR

VICEROY'S LODGE

FLAGSTAFF TOWER

St. STEPHEN'S COLLEGE

KINGSWAY CAMP

DELHI UNIVERSITY

MALL ROAD

CHATTRA MARG

UNIVERSITY ROAD

OLD SECRETARIAT

PIR GAIB

METCALF'S HOUSE

SHAMNATH MARG

RING ROAD

RIVER YAMUNA

ASHOKA PILLAR

HINDU RAO HOSPITAL

OBEROI MAIDENS

LUDLOW CASTLE

QUDSIA BAGH GATE

INTER STATE BUS TRML.

N

MUTINY MEMORIAL

QUDSIA BAGH MOSQUE

of solid stone, and on them Asoka carved his famous Edicts. They were made about 250 B.C. and are the oldest monuments in Delhi.

A little further along the road is a tall stone building and further on still an old mosque. These buildings belong to a palace which Firoz Shah Tughlaq built here about 1360. He came here to hunt and so built himself a hunting lodge or shikargah. It was called the **Kushk-i-shikar** and now is known as the **Pir Ghaib**.[1] There is another like it near the great tanks on the Ridge[2] behind New Delhi. From the palace an underground passage ran to the plain below. It is now blocked up because it has become unsafe.[3] It is just about here that Mallu Khan attacked Timur in 1398. Look over the Jumna and if the day is clear you will see in the distance a village on a small hill. This is Loni, where Timur's army encamped before he crossed the Jumna. It was then a flourishing town but is now only a village. You can reach it by the light railway from Shahdara. Look up the river and you will see the chimney of the pumping station at Wazirabad. That is where Timur crossed the Jumna with his army when he came to attack Delhi.

We will now look at some of the British monuments. Close by is Hindu Rao's house, now a hospital.[4] It was built by Sir Edward Colebrooke,[5] the Resident of Delhi. Then William Fraser lived in it. He was murdered when he was returning to this house from a party

---

[1] The appearance of the northern Ridge has changed considerably since Spear's time through the making of parks and general landscaping. The Chauburji (Four Domes) Masjid, which has since lost its domes, was outside the walled hunting lodge or palace. Nothing remains of the hunting lodge except the 'tall stone building' Spear refers to, which is the Pir Ghaib (Disappearing Mystic), named after a saint who suddenly dematerialized while meditating. The Pir Ghaib is now in the compound of the Hindu Rao Hospital.

[2] 'Tanks on the Ridge' refers to the Talkatora (see p. 82). The shikargah (hunting lodge) is a now ruined structure at the north end of the park.

[3] There are stories about tunnels attached to many Indian monuments. They are said to have linked palaces across Mughal cities, offering the rulers a private short cut or a place for secret assignations. Some may be based on fact but others, like the Britishers' supposed escape tunnel from Viceroy's House back to Britain, are presumably myths produced by the collective unconscious!

[4] The hospital occupies the site of Hindu Rao's house.

[5] See Spear, *Twilight of the Mughals*, for a vivid description of the 'Colebrooke Case'.

in 1835. The man who discovered the murderer was John Lawrence.[1] He was then a young man stationed at Panipat. After that Hindu Rao lived in the House for a long time. He was the brother of Baiza Bai, the famous Rani of Gwalior.[2] When her young son died in 1835 she had to leave Gwalior State. Hindu Rao went too, and he settled in Delhi and lived in this house. He lived in Delhi many years and was a very well-known character. From the Ridge you can also see a large house close to the river. This is the mansion built by Sir Thomas Metcalfe, which he lived in for many years. He was Commissioner of Delhi for eighteen years. He was the brother of Lord Metcalfe. He was a great admirer of Napoleon and had many books about him. He sent books to Napoleon when he was in exile at St Helena. Napoleon sent him back presents including his portrait. But the house and all its treasures were destroyed during the Mutiny by the Gujars. Before New Delhi was built, Metcalfe House was used for the Council of State. Now it is the headquarters of the Public Services Commission. Perhaps you will sit for your I.C.S. examination in its hall one day.[3]

The long white building with two towers is the old temporary secretariat.[4] The Legislative Assembly used to sit there and many famous men like Pt[5] Motilal Nehru, Pt Malaviya, and Mr Jinnah have sat and spoken there. On the other side of the Ridge you can see the Delhi University building. This was the Viceregal Lodge before the Viceroy's House was built in New Delhi.[6] Lord Hardinge, Lord

[1] John Lawrence, later Lord Lawrence, was Governor-General of India during 1864–69.

[2] After Daulat Rao Sindhia died in 1827 his widow, Baiza Bai, adopted a son, 'Janhoji'. She expected to rule in her own right but the British backed Janhoji and Baiza Bai was compelled to retire.

[3] Thomas Metcalfe was Agent and Commissioner during 1835–53. His much admired house is now part of the Defence Science Centre and not open to the public, but can be seen on the left from the Ring Road, travelling north. The Gujars resented the fact that their grazing lands had been appropriated for 'Matka Kothi' (Metcalfe/Water Jar House) and the house was badly damaged in 1857. The Indian Administrative Service (successor to the ICS) trained its officers in Metcalfe House until 1959, after which the Academy moved to Mussoorie.

[4] Now called the 'Old Secretariat', it houses the offices of the Legislative Assembly of the National Capital Region.

[5] Pandits ('Pt') Motilal Nehru (the father of Jawaharlal Nehru) and Malviya were leading members of the Congress Party, Jinnah of the Muslim League.

[6] A plaque in the Registrar's office marks where Lord Mountbatten proposed to Edwina Ashley.

Chelmsford, Lord Reading and Lord Irwin (now Lord Halifax)[1] have all lived there. Not far off is the house in which Mahatma Gandhi fasted for three weeks in 1924 because of communal rioting in Delhi.[2]

The British Army occupied the Ridge during the Mutiny through the hot weather and rains. Their camp was on the University grounds. There was much fighting in Sabzimundi[3] because Sabzimundi was the suburb of Delhi nearest to the Ridge.

Now we will go along Alipur Road.[4] At Timarpur we turn off and go to the river. Here[5] there is a fine bridge built by Firoz Shah, and a mosque where Shah Alam, a Muslim saint, is buried.

Coming back to Alipur Road we will drive on until we reach the main road at Azadpur. A mile further on is Badli-ki-serai. You can see the gateway of the old serai. This was a half stage from Delhi and travellers used to rest here on the first day of their journey to the north.[6] Leave the road on the left, walk between the serai and Badli village, cross the railway and you will see, half a mile away, a grove of trees. This is the famous Shalimar Garden of Delhi, which Shahjahan built. It is now a fruit garden, but you can walk about it, and find the central pavilion. There is also a lotus pond and an old waterfall. Aurangzeb stayed here when he was pursuing Dara Shikoh in 1658, and here he crowned himself Emperor of India. When the British came to Delhi the Resident Sir David Ochterlony and Lord Metcalfe used it as a country house. Once this garden was as fine as the Shalimar Garden at Lahore.[7]

[1] Lord Irwin (1926–31) was the last of these four Viceroys to live in the old Viceregal Lodge; he moved into Viceroy's House (now Rashtrapati Bhavan) on 23 December 1929 — in time for Christmas.

[2] The office of *The Comrade*, an English newspaper published by Maulana Mohammed Ali, who was a close associate of Mahatma Gandhi.

[3] Sabzi Mandi (Vegetable Market) was a large wholesale market, which was replaced in the 1970s by a new market further north, in Azadpur.

[4] Alipur Road is now also called Shamnath Marg.

[5] i.e. Wazirabad

[6] Badli-ki-serai, the site of an 1857 battle, is on the Grand Trunk Road (now Sher Shah Suri Marg).

[7] The original Shalimar Garden is in Srinagar, Kashmir, the biggest of the gardens laid out in Kashmir by the Mughals. Conceived by Jahangir, the name *Shala Mar* (Abode of Pleasure) was given by Shahjahan, who completed it and laid out further Shalimar Gardens in Lahore and Delhi. Ali Mardan Khan helped in the construction of the Delhi gardens (see Moynihan, *Paradise as a Garden*, pp. 125, 141–7). Sadly, since Spear wrote this, the surroundings have deteriorated still further and the garden

ADDITIONAL NOTES

Very little has been said about the Mutiny in this chapter. This is because all the facts are easily accessible in many books.

The British Army marched along the Grand Trunk road from Karnal. They defeated the mutineers at Badli-ki-serai, and then occupied the Ridge. Their camp was on the University site behind. It was protected by pickets on the little hills which are now being removed by the Improvement Trust.[1] Their rear was protected by the Najafgarh drain. On the other side there was a post on the mound near Metcalfe House. The sites of the batteries for the final bombardment are marked by inscriptions. You can get more details from Sharp's *Delhi* or Newell's *Three Days in Delhi*. A very good account of the siege is to be found in Fanshawe's *Delhi: Past and Present* (available in the Hardinge Library).[2] It is written by Lt (later Field Marshal) Norman, who was present at the siege. One of the best eye-witness accounts is by Lord Roberts.

Flagstaff Tower was built by the British. It was here that the English survivors waited on 11 May for the troops from Meerut who never came. The old magazine is still standing close to the river bank near Shah Alam's mosque at Wazirabad.[3] This contained great stores of ammunition and it was not blown up like the magazine in the city. It kept the mutineers supplied throughout the siege. The mutineers came from down country (Oudh) and were not Delhi men. They were called *Poorbeahs* because they came from the East.[4] All the evidence shows that they were heartily disliked and feared by the people of Delhi, and even by the emperor himself. The

---

is now hemmed in by housing estates.

[1] The Delhi Improvement Trust (DIT) was set up in 1937, after the A. P. Hume Report of 1936 had pointed out that there were crammed into Shahjahanabad 100,000 more people than it could possibly sustain. The DIT was superseded by the Delhi Development Authority (DDA) in 1957; the work of slum clearance was allotted to the Municipal Corporation (MCD). The New Delhi Municipal Committee (NDMC) controls Lutyens' New Delhi.

[2] The old *Hardinge* Library has been renamed the *Hardayal* Library, to commemorate Lala Har Dayal of Delhi (1884–1939), a scholar of Sanskrit and philosophy, and an ardent nationalist associated with the Ghadar (Revolt) Party.

[3] The mosque and bridge are at Wazirabad. The saint Shah Alam should not be confused with the two Mughal emperors of the same name.

[4] Poorb/purv (east) Awadh (not Oudh, the archaic British version), in eastern U.P., is 'down country' from Delhi, in Spear's unusual phrase, but it is more usual to talk about 'up country', meaning the areas north-west of Calcutta, which was the capital till 1912. The expression is chiefly used in northern India.

citizens of Delhi suffered very much from both sides. In wartime it is always the peaceful citizens who suffer most.

There is a new life of Charles, Lord Metcalfe, which tells us much about Delhi. It is by Edward Thompson. You should read it in your school library. There is another book by C.F. Andrews, called *Maulvi Zakaullah of Delhi*. It tells us much about the city before the Mutiny and you should read that also in your school library.[1]

---

[1] C. F. Andrews, who (like Spear) spent some years teaching at St Stephen's College, wrote this moving biography of a much revered scholar, teacher and reformer, who never lost his humility.

Part II

AROUND THE CITY

5. FIROZ SHAH KOTLA[1]

Firoz Shah was the last of the great Tughlaq kings who ruled Hindustan in the fourteenth century (1351–88). The first of them was Ghiyasuddin, who built Tughlaqabad. The second was Mohammed Shah, who built the palace near the Qutb, nowadays called the Bijay Mandal.[2] Mohammed Shah was a cruel and eccentric king who made all the citizens of Delhi move to Daulatabad in the Deccan and drove many others to revolt. Firoz Shah was his cousin. He succeeded to the throne when Mohammed died, while besieging the fortress of Thatta (near Karachi) in Sind. Firoz Shah led his army back to Delhi and then began to settle his kingdom. Firoz was a prudent and wise king, who thought of the good of his people. He was learned and pious. He loved peace and spent his revenues on public works instead of on waging more wars. On the whole the people were happier under his rule than they had been for a long time. One of the best things that Firoz Shah did was to dig the canal which nowadays we call the Western Jumna Canal. It started from the Jumna near Karnal and one branch came to Delhi and one branch went to Hissar and Sirsa. The canal used to be broader than it is now. If you go along the Western Jumna Canal from Delhi for a few miles you will see one of the banks which Firoz built, running parallel to the present canal banks. This canal brought water for the peasants so that their crops grew even if the monsoons failed. Later on the canal was damaged and the water ceased to run until Shahjahan repaired it again. The officer who did this was Ali Mardan Khan and so the canal came to be called Ali Mardan's Canal.[3] When Ahmad Shah Abdali took

---

[1] Kotla is the diminutive of Kot (fort), and means a citadel, or fortified area within a city. See pp. 27–8 and pp. 104–5 for more on Tughlaq architecture in general.

[2] See pp. 70–2 for more on the Bijay Mandal.

[3] Canals have been used to irrigate Delhi since at least the thirteenth century. There are three major ones, two west of the Yamuna, and one east:

– Firoz Shah Tughlaq's canal, from Safidun (west of Panipat) to his hunting lodge on the north Delhi ridge.

– The Nahar-i-Behisht, from Khizrabad, 20 km north of Saharanpur, through

Delhi the canal was ruined again, but in 1820 the British repaired it and ever since the water has flowed freely. So Firoz Shah was a great benefactor of the people.

Firoz Shah Kotla. Firoz Shah was very fond of building, so when he had settled his affairs, he decided to build a new palace. There were already three royal palaces, one at Siri, one at Bijay Mandal, and one at the Qutb.[1] But Firoz Shah decided to build another by the banks of the Jumna, where he could feel the cool breezes from the mountains and the river. So he built Firoz Shah Kotla and called it Firozabad. When you enter the gate today, the big open space on the left, which is now a green lawn, was the public part of the palace. On the right are the halls of public and private audience. On the left of the big lawn is a deep *baoli*, where the king used to cool himself in hot weather. Near here Alamgir II was murdered in 1759 by the order of his minister Imadulmulk.[2]

Asoka's pillar. On the other side of the palace is a great mosque which was the Jama Masjid of Firoz Shah's time. It has no fine ornament now, but look at its fine and noble proportions. Close to the mosque is a building with a pillar on top of it. This building was part of the private apartments of the king, and the pillar is Asoka's pillar. The pillar was originally erected by Asoka near Ambala in 250 B.C. Firoz Shah found it when hunting, and as he liked old monuments, he transported it to Delhi on a great carriage with forty-two wheels. Hundreds of men were employed to drag it. It used to have

---

Panipat to Shahjahanabad, built reputedly by Ali Mardan Khan, who had also constructed a canal near Lahore.

– The Eastern Jumna Canal (early eighteenth century) also from Khizrabad to east Delhi. Unfortunately, over a period of time, irrigation from the Canals caused salinity in the fields and they were abandoned. The British repaired them in 1820 but the salinity recurred. The canals' channels can be seen in Defence Colony, between C and D blocks, and cutting the Outer Ring Road north to south at Panchsheel Park, near the Chiragh Delhi flyover.

Incidentally, the Nehru family's name was derived from its canal connections: 'Our family migrated to Delhi in 1716. A jagir with a house situated on the banks of a canal had been granted to Raj Kaul and "Nehru" (from *nahar*, a canal) came to be attached to his name. Kaul had been the family name. This changed to Kaul Nehru and in later years we became simply Nehru' (Jawaharlal Nehru, *An Autobiography*, p.1).

[1] There was yet another palace at Kilokheri, near present-day Maharani Bagh.

[2] Imadulmulk was the title of Ghaziuddin Khan III, the great-grandson of Ghaziuddin Khan I, who founded the *madarsa* referred to on p. 11.

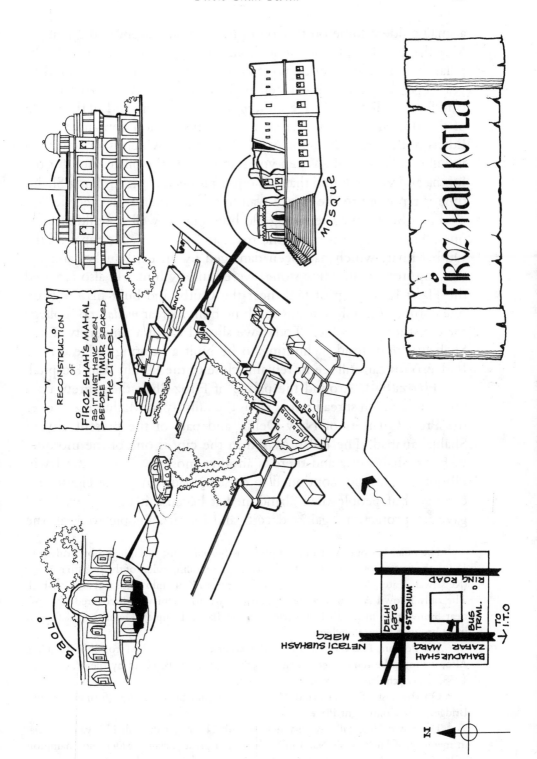

RECONSTRUCTION OF FIROZ SHAH'S MAHAL AS IT MUST HAVE BEEN BEFORE TIMUR SACKED THE CITADEL.

Mosque

Baoli

FIROZ SHAH KOTLA

NETAJI SUBHASH MARG
DELHI GATE
STADIUM
RING ROAD
BAHADUR SHAH ZAFAR MARG
BUS TRML.
TO I.T.O

N

a small golden dome on the top of it, but that disappeared when the Marathas and Jats plundered Delhi in the eighteenth century. On the pillar there is an inscription which nobody could read until a hundred years ago, because it is written in Pali, the sacred language of the Buddhists. Pali is a language something like Sanskrit, and all the books of the Buddhists are written in it.[1] The inscription contains various Edicts of the great Emperor Asoka, the first of which is an order not to kill certain animals. When you stand beside the pillar, look for the Jumna and you will find that it is quite a long way off. In Firoz Shah's time it ran close to the palace wall, but since then it has receded.

Firoz Shah loved repairing old buildings as well as building new ones. Therefore he is called the royal archaeologist. He repaired the Qutb Minar, which had been damaged by an earthquake, and the two top storeys (in white stone) were built by him. He also repaired the Hauz Khas, a great tank near the Qutb, and built his tomb on one corner of it. Close to his tomb he built a great *madarsa* or college for the study of Arabic.[2] Today we should call it a university. Firoz Shah was very fond of hunting so he built a hunting lodge on the Ridge. You can still see its remains close to the Hindu Rao Hospital.

Firozabad. Around the palace of Firoz Shah there grew up a great city, which spread out as far as the railway to Mathura, and over the Press Quarters of New Delhi[3] and part of the present city of Shahjahanabad. The Kalan Masjid in the city is one of the mosques of Firoz Shah's city and there is another mosque close to the Irwin Hospital.[4] This city continued to exist right down to the eighteenth century, but people then abandoned it because it had no wall and gave no protection against dacoits and looters. People took all the

[1] The pillar has one Asokan inscription in *Brahmi* script (deciphered by Prinsep in 1836); the rest are of later date in the *kutila* script, extolling rulers of the twelfth century (Kejariwal). Later, Akbar shifted an Asoka pillar from Kausambi to his fort at Allahabad. The only known Asokan *rock* inscription original to Delhi was discovered in 1967, near Srinivaspuri in South Delhi (close to the Bahai Temple); Delhi's Asoka *pillars* were brought from elsewhere.

[2] Also Persian. This was only one of the *madarsas* established by Firoz Shah Tughlaq. Also, it should be remembered that after the capture of Baghdad by the Mongols in 1258, many scholars fled from there to Delhi.

[3] On the east of Vivekanand Marg, just beyond Sivaji Bridge (formerly Minto Bridge) near Connaught Place.

[4] The Irwin Hospital was renamed the Lok Nayak Jai Prakash Narayan Hospital in memory of Jai Prakash Narayan (1902–79), a great socialist leader and champion of landless rural labourers. 'Lok Nayak' means 'People's Leader'.

stones of the houses away so that now only the palace and the mosques are left.[1] Firoz Shah died in 1388, at the age of 90. Except for Aurangzeb, he was the oldest of all the Kings of Delhi. Ten years later Timur came and destroyed the Tughlaq empire.

ADDITIONAL NOTES

The style of the Tughlaq period has certain very distinctive features which enable it to be very easily distinguished.

(i)   It is very heavy and massive. The walls of the buildings often slope outwards and remind one of the buildings of ancient Egypt. This gives the impression of great strength. *Examples:* Tughlaqabad. Tomb of Ghiyasuddin Tughlaq.

(ii) The material used is the plain local stone. This was covered with plaster, but often the plaster has peeled off and only the stone is left without any ornament. The only important Tughlaq building with red stone and white marble is the tomb of Ghiyasuddin Tughlaq at Tughlaqabad. We do not know the reasons for this for certain, but we may suggest two possibilities.

(a)   The whole revenue of the empire was used in repressing the constant rebellions and the Deccan campaigns.

(b)   After Mohammed Tughlaq removed the inhabitants of Delhi to Daulatabad skilled stonemasons were lacking. Both before and after this time red stone and marble were used, so this is a good indication. *Example:* Firoz Shah Kotla.

(iii) All Tughlaq buildings employ the true arch with a key-stone (explained elsewhere).[2] *Example:* Tughlaqabad.

---

[1] Shahjahan was the chief culprit, cannibalizing the building blocks of Firozabad to build his own city just to the north (see Fanshawe, *Delhi: Past and Present*, p. 226), but he was merely continuing a long tradition: Humayun had laid the first brick of Dinpanah using one raided from Siri, and Sher Shah used the bricks of Firozabad and Dinpanah to construct his own Shergarh on a site which included parts of each city. (Just like children playing with building bricks — not even pausing to admire their playmate's efforts before knocking them down to create their own model town.) In the emperors' defence, however, it must be pointed out that they were not simply vandals: each incoming ruler was expected to institute an extensive building programme in order to maintain full employment of his people, and in Islam it is an act of piety to found a city (see *The Cambridge History of Islam*, p. 446).

[2] See pp. 102–3 for more on keystones and true arches.

(iv)　The Tughlaqs built pillars in their arches and verandahs in the Hindu style, i.e. one slab of stone is laid horizontally across two upright slabs to form the door or pillar.

(v)　The proportions of the buildings are always fine for all their sternness. *Example* : Mosque at Firoz Shah Kotla.

In general, any building which is rough and heavy but well proportioned and which uses pillars for its doors and verandahs, is likely to be a Tughlaq building. These indications will enable you to tell for certain. Remember these points and as you go about try to identify the different styles.

Examples of the Tughlaq period worth visiting : Firoz Shah Kotla, Kalan Masjid, Khirki Masjid (two miles from the Qutb), Hauz Khas, Bijay Mandal, Tughlaqabad and the tomb of Ghiyasuddin Tughlaq.

6. PURANA QILA

The Purana Qila[1] stands on the site of the city of Indraprastha. Indraprastha is the first city of Delhi and was the capital of the Pandavas in the great war of the *Mahabharata*. The Purana Qila was probably the palace or citadel of Indraprastha and the houses of the city extended over the plain between the Purana Qila and Humayun's tomb.[2] We do not know for certain that this is so, but it is quite likely. All the other cities of the Pandavas — Baghpat, Tilpat, Sonepat and Panipat — are known, and Indraprastha is quite near to them. We do not know for certain because there are no buildings left from those times. The reason for this is that in those days men built their houses of mud and their palaces of wood, which have all been burnt

[1] Humayun called the city he began Dinpanah (Refuge of the Faithful). See p.26 for more on this city which he shares the credit for with Sher Shah Suri, who referred to it as Shergarh. Even after Shahjahanabad was built, the citadel of Dinpanah continued as a centre of population for some time, just as Mehrauli had: the earlier Delhis were not abandoned in nomadic fashion unless, for example, the water supply ran out. Dinpanah therefore became known as Purana Qila (Old Fort) to distinguish it from the Lal Qila (Red Fort) of Shahjahanabad, which was finished in 1648. This is a continuing process of course: what the British called Old Delhi was always Mehrauli, until the construction of British New Delhi, after which Shahjahanabad became Old Delhi. And now British New Delhi in turn is in danger of being eclipsed by Highrise New Delhi. *Sic transit gloria mundi!*

[2] Spear's imagination has here telescoped time so that Delhi's historical cities exist concurrently rather than consecutively, making Yudhisthira and Indraprastha co-exist with Humayun and Purana Qila and even Lutyens' War Memorial.

or carried away by later people. You can imagine King Yudhisthira holding his court in the Purana Qila, and all the busy life of a great city going on around. You can imagine the heroes riding in on their horses, or driving out to battle in their chariots. Perhaps they drove over the ground where the War Memorial Arch[1] now is when they went out to the great battle of Kurukshetra.

Remember that there is nothing now left of ancient Indraprastha. The walls you now see were built long after and we know nothing about what happened here in all the time between. The present Purana Qila was begun by the Emperor Humayun in 1530 A.D..[2] He wanted to build a new capital for the Mughal dynasty. So when his father Babur died, he came to Delhi and chose this site. The river Jumna flowed close by in those days — where the station of Nizamuddin is now. So Humayun could enjoy the breezes from the river in the hot weather. Humayun built a great city as well. One of the gates of the city is still left. It stands opposite the gaol[3] and is called the **Khuni Darwaza**. You can see it as you drive out of the Delhi gate.

But Humayun did not finish his new city. In 1540 Sher Shah Suri, the Afghan, defeated him on the Ganges and he fled away to Persia. Sher Shah became the Emperor of Hindustan and he reigned for five years. He finished both the Purana Qila and the city and lived there during his reign. That is why the buildings inside the Purana Qila are called after Sher Shah.

Now we will go inside the Purana Qila. Enter by the gate which faces the Mathura road[4] and walk along the path inside. First you will

[1] The All-India War Memorial, 'always called India Gate by the Indians because the word India was carved on the entablature' (see Nirad Chaudhuri p. 723), faces Rashtrapati Bhavan at the end of Raj Path, over 2 km away. The alignment is so good that the statue of George V in his canopy could clearly be seen through the middle of the Memorial arch by the Viceroy from his house on top of Raisina Hill.

[2] Humayun actually laid the foundation of Dinpanah in July 1533.

[3] The gaol no longer exists but the site, now surrounded by the campus of the Maulana Azad Medical College, has become a memorial (called Shahid Sthal) to those imprisoned here for political offences at the time of the nationalist movement.

[4] On the Mathura Road is the western or Bara (Big) Darwaza (Gate) used by visitors. Visible from the Crafts Museum, the beautiful northern or Talaqi (Forbidden) Darwaza has been closed since, according to Hearn (p.127), 'some king ordered it to be shut behind him as he went out to battle and never to be opened unless he returned victorious'. Perhaps this refers to 1545 when, on one of his numerous forays from the city to wage battle in the hinterland, 'King' Sher Shah was killed during the siege of Kalanjar. From the southern gate there is a striking view back to Humayun's Tomb,

see, in the middle of the Qila, a very deep well. This was built by Humayun in order that the fort should always have water. It is a very deep well because the Fort stands on a hill. Beyond the well you will see on your left hand a mosque. This is Sher Shah's mosque.[1] This is one of the most beautiful mosques built in Delhi before the time of the Mughals. Notice the carving and the arches, the roof and the Arabic texts. Notice also the different kinds of stone which are used, and their different colours. They are red and white and grey and black, and they make the mosque very beautiful. Lord Curzon repaired this mosque and the Amir Habibullah of Afghanistan repaired the tank in the courtyard.[2]

The other building inside the Purana Qila is the **Sher Mandal**. It is an octagonal (eight-sided) building, and has very steep steps[3] leading up to the roof. This building was built by Sher Shah like the mosque. But after Sher Shah had died, Humayun came back to India and recovered his empire in 1555. He marched to Delhi and made it his capital once more. Humayun loved art and learning and philosophy and he liked to discuss these things with poets and learned men. So he used this building as a library in which to keep his books, and you can still see some of the shelves in which he kept them.[4]

---

through which one can imagine the emperor even now wistfully keeping watch on the city he founded but barely lived to enjoy.

[1] See more on Sher Shah's mosque (Qila-i-Kuhna Masjid) on p. 32 and p. 106.

[2] Amir Habibullah visited India from 2 January – 7 March 1907 as a guest of the Viceroy, Lord Minto.

[3] Why are the steps of many historic Delhi monuments so steep? Dignified, emperor-like progression up and down would have been impossible and in every other way these rulers prided themselves on the art of living well. In some cases, such as Ghiyasuddin Tughlaq's tomb (which also housed a treasury), the difficult access is a good defence, as you will discover for yourself if you try storming it! In Mughal monuments, Ebba Koch has suggested that, for aesthetic reasons, the architect needed to keep the stairs within the width of the wall and they were therefore necessarily steep. Philippa Vaughan points out that there was no tradition of procession through their courts by Mughal emperors (as their European equivalents would have done); at certain times of day the emperor appeared in his *jharoka*, but his procession *to* the *jharoka* was not a court appearance. It may also be that the steepness of the steps themselves was intended to inspire in the visitor a due sense of awe at the grandeur of the place and its inhabitants. Mediaeval pilgrims to France's Rocamadour traditionally climbed the long stone steps on their knees; this was of course an act of *religious* homage, but the modern tourist in India occasionally feels a belated sense of sympathy!

[4] Sadly the library interior is now closed to visitors, though it can be seen in the

One day in January 1556, Humayun was sitting on the roof of the Sher Mandal, enjoying the afternoon sun. He heard the call to prayer and hurried down the steep stone steps. On one of these he slipped and hurt himself so badly that he died soon after. You can still see one step which is broken and it is said that it was on this step that Humayun slipped. Akbar succeeded his father Humayun as emperor and lived in Delhi for a few years. Then he decided to build a city of his own and went away to Agra. Between the Sher Mandal and Sher Shah's mosque are some low brick buildings. These are the remains of the *hammam* or royal baths.

Notice, as you go outside, the beautiful carving of the gateways of the Purana Qila. Just as in Sher Shah's mosque, so in the gateway, different kinds of stone are used with different colours. The colours blend or mix together, and give a beautiful effect.[1]

Outside the Purana Qila and on the other side of the road is a mosque and college or madarsa. This was built by Maham Anaga, the foster-mother of Akbar, who ruled the empire for some time when Akbar was a boy.

ADDITIONAL NOTES

The mistake which is commonly made with regard to the Purana Qila is to think that the walls are those of the ancient Indraprastha. This is impossible because the people of those times only used wood for their important buildings. We do know, however, that the site is a very ancient one. Archaeologists have found remains of the Gupta period (4th century A.D..) and it is quite possible that some day, if excavation is carried deep enough, traces of the Indus valley culture will be discovered. [2]

Granada TV series 'The Great Mughals' by Bamber Gascoigne. For an account of the Mughals' libraries, see Brand and Lowry, *Akbar's India*, Ch. 3, 'The Kitabkhana: The Imperial Library').

[1] The massive gateways are of stone. The *chhatris* are inset with well-preserved coloured tiles.

[2] 'India owes the introduction of the use of stone for architectural purposes . . . to the great Asoka. . . . Like the buildings of the Burmese at the present day, [their buildings] were all in wood' (Fergusson, *Indian and Eastern Architecture*, vol 1, p. 51). The Purana Qila is on a mound where there have been successive settlements. The popular name of the site, Indrapat (Indraprastha, City of Lord Indra), suggests that it was one of the five villages given to the Pandavas as recounted in the *Mahabharata*, dating from

Sher Shah's mosque is, with the Moth-ki-masjid near the Qutb road,[1] the finest building of the pre-Mughal Lodi style of architecture.[2] Note specially:

(i)   How the different kinds of stone, Delhi stone, red sandstone, black and white marble are combined so as to make a beautiful colour scheme.

(ii)   How the pointed arch (a Muslim feature) is combined with Hindu brackets and ornaments and the horizontal arch.

(iii)   The perfect proportions of the buildings.

The Lodi style represents, as Sir John Marshall says, a perfect union of the characteristic features of the Hindu and Muslim styles.[3] It is a permanent symbol of Hindu–Muslim unity.

The building next to Maham Anaga's mosque is a bazaar belonging to Sher Shah's city. The Khuni Darwaza (opposite the gaol) gets its name from the fact that executions took place there at the time of the Mutiny.[4]

7. HUMAYUN'S TOMB

Humayun's tomb is one of the most beautiful Mughal monuments. There are many other interesting buildings all round it. In the days of the great Mughals, Humayun's tomb was in a suburb of the city. Near it was the shrine of Nizamuddin to which people went, as they do today. Probably for this reason many nobles built their tombs here. Humayun's widow and the mother of Akbar, Hamida Banu Begum,

---

the first millennium B.C. Excavations carried out after 1955 showed remains of a settlement of the 2nd c. B.C. (See Y.D. Sharma, *Delhi and its Neighbourhood*, plate XXI). These finds are now displayed in the Purana Qila museum (to the right of the main entrance).

[1] This road is now Aurobindo Marg.

[2] 'Under the Lodis, a new type of [small, single-aisled mosque] developed, one that ultimately became a major type in Mughal India' (C. Asher's *Architecture of Mughal India*, p. 11).

[3] John Marshall, 'The Monuments of Muslim India', *The Cambridge History of India*, vol. III (Cambridge, 1922).

[4] Originally the Kabul Darwaza of Sher Shah's city, it was renamed Khuni Darwaza (Bloodstained Gateway) after 1857, because it was here that Captain Hodson shot four Mughal princes imprisoned after the siege of Delhi. It is in the middle of Bahadur Shah Zafar Marg near Firoz Shah Kotla. Opposite it is the little Masjid Mehndian, where the renowned scholars and reformers, Maulana Shah Wali-ulla (d. 1764) and his son, Maulana Shah Abdul Aziz (d. 1824), lie buried.

built this tomb in 1565 A.D..[1] Humayun's tomb is six miles from Shahjahanabad, which is a half-day's march. So many people, when they set out on a journey along Akbar's Grand Trunk Road to Agra, stayed here for the first night, instead of going a full stage the first day.[2]

When you go to Humayun's tomb today you will first come to a tomb with a blue dome. The road makes a circle round it. The dome is made of tiles from Persia.[3] The people of Delhi did not know about these blue tiles until the Mughals came to India. They brought the tiles with them and started a new fashion.

When you turn in to Humayun's tomb, you will see on the right an enclosure with a tomb and a mosque. This is the tomb and the mosque of Isa Khan. Isa Khan was one of the nobles of Sher Shah, and died a few years before Humayun came back to Delhi. The tomb is very beautiful but you will see that it is very different from Humayun's tomb.[4]

Now we will come to Humayun's tomb itself. First we go through an archway and along a path to another gateway. This archway is not the real entrance to Humayun's tomb. It is a part of a garden which belonged to a Mughal noble, but which has now disappeared.[5] As you walk along the path to the real gate of Humayun's tomb, you

[1] Elsewhere the credit is given to Humayun's *senior* widow, Bega Begum, called Haji Begum (because she had performed the *haj*). The architect she commissioned was Mirak Mirza Ghiyas, from Herat who 'provided India with her first dome in the Persian tradition' (Gascoigne, *The Great Moghuls*, p. 99). She died in 1581; Hamida Banu died shortly before Akbar, in 1603, and was 'buried, with great ceremony' in Humayun's mausoleum. She was called Mariam Makani by Akbar, in distinction to Mariam *Zamani*, his wife.

[2] The Grand Trunk Road has a long ancestry. It was the route from Pataliputra (Patna) to Gandhara, in Afghanistan, during the Mauryan empire (third century B.C.); it was extended to East Bengal (Sonargaon) by Sher Shah; in 1836 it was repaired and linked to Calcutta by the British, and it became the backbone of their Indian empire.(See Rudyard Kipling, *Kim*, for an evocative account of The Road.) Its Delhi section is now called Sher Shah Suri Marg.

[3] Although the tiles are blue, this late sixteenth century or early seventeenth century tomb, a Baghdadi octagon, is called the Sabz Burj (Green Dome). Its dome was re-tiled in a vivid blue by the ASI in the 1980s; only the tiles on the drum below the dome (in a mosaic of green, blue and yellow) are original. Cf. p. 107, n.1, below.

[4] The point is that Isa Khan's tomb, built in 1547–48, was an octagonal tomb, like those of Sher Shah Suri in Sasaram and the Lodis and Sayyids in Delhi. Humayun's Tomb is the first important *Mughal* monument in India.

[5] Bu Halima's garden.

will see on your right another large archway. This is the entrance to a great serai, where people used to rest on their way from Delhi. It is called the Arab serai, and was built by Hamida Banu Begum in 1560–1 for 300 Arabs she had brought back with her from Mecca.[1] Inside the gateway you will see a lot of ruins and also many graves.

Now we come to the gateway of Humayun's tomb.[2] When we go inside we see that we are in a large square enclosure. In the centre is Humayun's tomb itself. It stands on a great stone platform.[3] From the tomb in the middle of each side run stone channels. These channels were filled with water, which kept the garden green and fresh. In between the water-channels there are trees and grass. The Mughal gardeners built little canals all over these spaces, as the malis do today in our gardens. Along the big stone canals they planted flowers. Some of the flowers bloomed by day like the roses, some bloomed by night like the jasmine, so that whenever anyone came to the garden there were beautiful flowers to look at. In between the big canals were planted small trees. Some of them were fruit trees like pomegranates, and some of them were flowering trees like the gold mohur and the *amaltas*.[4] So whether it was hot or cold weather, day or night, there were always beautiful trees and flowers to look at. The Mughals loved gardens and always made them wherever they went. They loved gardens so much that whenever they built a tomb they always built a garden as well. The noblemen who built the tomb used it as a pleasure pavilion for his family as long as he lived.

Now we come to the tomb itself. You will see that it is built on a great stone platform. This was a new idea of the Mughals and all their tombs are built like this. Then notice the stone. It is red sandstone with a white marble dome. These stones were very expensive, but

[1] Or *Persian* artisans working on the tomb?

[2] Today the western gate is the 'main' one, but earlier it was the southern gate that was used.

[3] See pp. 36–7, 106–8 and Afterword for more on the architectural significance of Humayun's Tomb.

[4] The *gul* (flower) *mohur* (Persian gold coin) — *Poinciana regia* — is a tall umbrella-like tree, a native of Madagascar. In May it is a brilliant mass of scarlet-gold flowers. The *amaltas* (Indian laburnum) is a small tree, which in May is also laden with golden cascades of flowers. M.S. Randhawa, the distinguished civil servant and botanist, commented, 'Foreigners who happen to see an amaltas or a gulmohur in bloom wonder at our neglect of such splendid material for beautifying our country. Why have we made no use of this wealth of rich colours?'

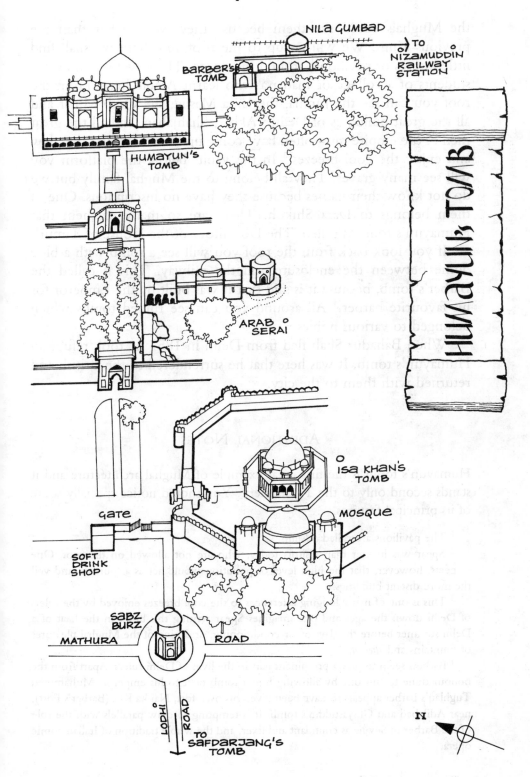

the Mughals could use them because they were richer than the previous kings. We will go up to the roof and there we shall find little houses or pavilions[1] around the dome. These were used by the students of a college or madarsa who learnt Arabic here. From the roof you can see the Jumna, the Jama Masjid, the Qutb Minar and all the great buildings of Delhi.[2] Akbar, Shahjahan, and all the great men of the empire must often have come up here to admire the view and enjoy the cool breezes.[3] In the vaults below the platform you will see many graves. They all belong to the Mughal family but we do not know their names because they have no inscriptions. One of them belongs to Dara Shikoh. There are so many of them that Humayun's tomb is called 'The Dormitory of the House of Timur'.

If you look back from the roof you will see a tomb with a blue dome between the enclosure and the railway. This is called the Barber's tomb, because it is said that it was built by the Emperor for his favourite barber.[4] All around you can see ruined tombs which belonged to various nobles.

When Bahadur Shah fled from Delhi in 1857 he took refuge in Humayun's tomb. It was here that he surrendered to the British and returned with them to the city.

ADDITIONAL NOTES

Humayun's tomb is the first great example of Mughal architecture and it stands second only to the Taj in merit. You should notice specially some of its principal features.

[1] The pavilions are called *chhattris*.

[2] Spear was luckier than visitors today, who are not allowed on the roof. One suspects, however, that the high level of pollution would act as a 'purdah' and veil the more distant buildings.

[3] This is one of many longing references to the cool breezes enjoyed by the rulers of Delhi down the ages and one imagines Spear writing this book in the heat of a Delhi summer before the days of air-conditioning, dreaming of the Mughal pleasures of fountains and *sherbet*.

[4] Barbers seem to play a prominent part in the lives of Delhi rulers. Apart from the honour done to this one by allowing him a tomb next to his emperor, Muhammed Tughlaq's barber appears to have been given his own fort, Nai ka Kot (Barber's Fort), near Adilabad and Ghiyasuddin's tomb. It is tempting to draw parallels with the role of the Barber of Seville as confidant and fixer, and the whole tradition of Italian comic opera.

(i) Notice that the tomb is placed on a large stone platform. This is quite a new idea and makes the tomb more imposing.

(ii) The materials (red sandstone and marble) are richer than those of previous buildings. This is because the Mughals were far richer than the Lodis or the Suris.

(iii) The dome is what is called a *full* dome. That is, it is a complete semicircle. All Mughal domes were full domes, and all previous domes were half-domes, or only half a semicircle. On the top of the dome there is just a crescent, but no lotus. This is because the architect was a Persian. The later Mughal domes (e.g. the Taj) have the lotus.

(iv) Notice the carved texts and inlaid work on the marble on the walls. It is very beautiful.

(v) Notice also the *jali* or trellis work in red sandstone. This is a special Mughal feature and reaches its greatest perfection in the time of Shahjahan.

8. NIZAMUDDIN

Everyone knows Nizamuddin. Very likely you have been there already. Perhaps you went to a *mela* there. Perhaps you went to see the saint's tomb. Or perhaps you have seen it from a distance.[1] You have all heard of Kh. Hasan Nizami. He claims to be the direct descendant of Sheikh Nizamuddin Chisti and lives close to the shrine. Nizamuddin's tomb is not only a holy place where the saint lies buried. It is also a famous place where many famous people are also buried. Famous men liked to be buried there because they wanted to lie near to so famous a saint.

---

[1] 'Everyone knows Nizamuddin' — Hazrat Nizamuddin Auliya (b. Badayun 1236, d. Delhi 1325) was a humanitarian Sufi and mystic whose *khanqah* has continuously attracted people from many places, many backgrounds and different religions. This place came to acquire the saint's name. 'During his lifetime a saint exudes *baraka* [spiritual power] and this continued to emanate from his grave' (James Dickie in Michell, p. 44). Today it is known as Nizamuddin Basti (west of Mathura Road). Nizamuddin East is across the Mathura Road, near the railway station named Hazrat Nizamuddin. Melas are held twice a year, in April and October, at Nizamuddin Basti, on the occasion of the *Urs* (anniversary celebrations) of Hazrat Nizamuddin Auliya and Amir Khusrau (see p. 39, note 3). Today the complex can be seen from the Lodhi/Oberoi Hotel flyover. N.B. 'Basti', meaning inhabited quarter, is used for the old section of the town.

When you enter the shrine of Nizamuddin you come first to a tank. Nizamuddin himself built this tank in the reign of Ghiyasuddin Tughlaq. He quarrelled with Ghiyas about it. Ghiyasuddin was building Tughlaqabad and wanted all the workmen for the great walls. But they preferred to work for the saint and defied the great king. Ghiyas was in Bengal when he heard the news, and vowed that he would punish the saint when he returned. Nizamuddin's friends asked him to flee away before the king returned. But always the saint replied *'Delhi hanuz dur ast'*.[1] At last Ghiyas came to Afghanpur, one day's march from Delhi. But there a pavilion fell on him and killed him, so Nizamuddin escaped his vengeance.[2]

When you enter the gateway of Nizamuddin's shrine you come first to a tank.[3] Passing by the tank you come into a courtyard where stands the tomb of Nizamuddin. The grave itself was built at the saint's death but the rest of the building is later. Shahjahan added the marble arches which surround the grave, and which are very beautiful, and Akbar II built the dome. On one side of the tomb is a very beautiful mosque called the Jama'at Khana,[4] built in the time of Alauddin Khilji, and it was perhaps on account of this mosque that Nizam chose this spot for his tank and his residence. Around the courtyard of the tomb is a marble screen or *jali* which Shahjahan built. You should look at it carefully because the work is very fine. It is just like the marble work in Delhi palace[5] and in Shahjahan's palace at Agra.

Around the shrine of Nizamuddin are so many tombs and buildings that it would take all day to see them.[6] So I shall only tell you of some of the most important and interesting ones.

[1] 'Delhi is yet far off' (see Afterword on Tughlaqabad for more on this fascinating story).

[2] See also Chapter 18 Tughlaqabad (p. 80).

[3] The tank is called '*Chashma dilkusha*' (Delightful Spring).

[4] The Jama'at Khana (Assembly Room) is also described on p. 42.

[5] 'Delhi palace' here means the Red Fort.

[6] 'Historical knowledge shall remain beholden to Khwaja Hasan Nizami, himself a renowned Sufi and man of letters, for the sincere efforts he made to identify and preserve the graves in the area. . . . The graves that have sprung up from 1325 to the present day round the mausoleum of the Sheikh are like seals of history attesting to the feelings of love and faith which the Sheikh has enjoyed. . . . His life-story . . . provides a happy diversion from the pomp and panoply of the medieval courts and the din and clatter of the battlefields' (Khaliq Ahmed Nizami, *Life and Times of Shaikh Nizamuddin Auliya*, pp. 180–1). His son, Kh. or Khwaja Hasan Sani (Second) Nizami, is the present *pirzada* (custodian of the shrine).

I. The grave of Jahanara

Princess Jahanara[1] lies in a little marble enclosure on one side of Nizam's courtyard. She has a marble head-stone and nothing but the green grass upon her grave. She was the best of the Mughal princesses and her grave is the most simple and beautiful of them all. For many years she was the Padshah Begum of Shahjahan's court. When Aurangzeb imprisoned his father, Shahjahan, at Agra she voluntarily shared his captivity for eight years until he died. Before she died she wrote her own epitaph which you can read in Persian on her tombstone:

> Let nought but the green grass cover the grave of Jahanara
> For grass is the fittest covering for the tomb of the lowly.

As she wrote, so it was; and the green grass still grows upon her grave.[2]

II. The tomb of Amir Khusrau[3]

Amir Khusrau was the greatest of all the poets of Delhi. He lived in the reign of Alauddin and was a great friend of his artistic son Khizr Khan.[4] He wrote about Khizr Khan's exploits. But Alauddin grew jealous of his son and at last imprisoned him. But his evil deed lived after him. Soon he died, his foolish son Mubarak[5] was murdered, and his dynasty was overthrown.

---

[1] Princess Jahanara was the favourite daughter of Shahjahan.

[2] Like Christina Rossetti:

> Be the green grass above me with flowers and dewdrops wet.
> And if thou wilt, remember, and if thou wilt, forget.

Her grave is usually strewn with rose petals.

[3] Amir Khusrau (1253–1325) was court poet to seven Delhi Sultans, a singer and musicologist who is said to have invented the sitar. He was also a mystic and disciple of Nizamuddin.

[4] Khizr Khan, son of Alauddin Khilji, married Dewal Devi, daughter of the Raja of Gujarat. Khusrau wrote a heroic poem of their love called *Ashiqa* or *Dewal Rani Khizr Khan*, in 1319.

[5] Mubarak Shah became Sultan in 1317. He killed Khizr Khan and himself married his widow, Dewal Devi. Khusrau wrote *Nuh Sipihr* in his honour. Mubarak was in turn murdered by his Wazir in 1321.

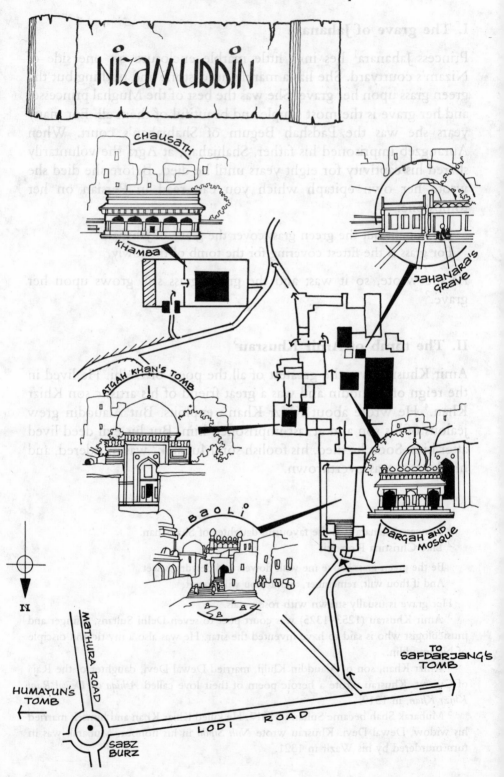

NIZAMUDDIN

CHAUSATH

KHAMBA

JAHANARA'S
GRAVE

ATGAH KHAN'S TOMB

BAOLI

DARGAH AND
MOSQUE

N

MATHURA ROAD

TO
SAFDARJANG'S
TOMB

HUMAYUN'S
TOMB

SABZ
BURZ

LODI   ROAD

Amir Khusrau's tomb is just beyond Jahanara's, and stands within an enclosure crowded with the tombs of princes and nobles.

III. The tomb of Ghalib

Just outside the gate of Nizamuddin's shrine is a little cemetery with a few simple graves. One of these is that of the poet Ghalib.[1] He has an inscription in Persian which you can read for yourself. Not all great men have mighty tombs, and this plain stone covers the remains of one of the greatest of Delhi's sons. Ghalib was the greatest Urdu poet of the nineteenth century. He was a friend of Bahadur Shah and was the rival of the Court poet Zauq. Stand with reverence before this stone, for here lies the Urdu Shakespeare.

IV. The tomb of Atgah Khan

Close to the grave of Ghalib stands the tomb of Atgah Khan. It is built of red stone and has a fine marble dome.[2] Atgah Khan was a foster-father of Akbar. When he grew up he was a great friend of Akbar, but Adham Khan, the son of Maham Anaga, Akbar's foster-mother,[3] who ruled the empire for Akbar, became jealous of him. One day they quarrelled, and Adham Khan killed Atgah. He rushed into Akbar's private apartments with the blood on his hands. Akbar jumped up in a rage, seized Adham, carried him across the terrace and threw him over with his own hands.[4] From that day Akbar deposed Maham Anaga and ruled himself.

---

[1] Mirza Asadullah Khan 'Ghalib' (1797–1869) was, with Mir Taqi Mir, the greatest *ghazal* poet. He wrote in both Urdu and Persian and, after the death of Zauq in 1854, was appointed *ustaad* (teacher) to Bahadur Shah II, who wrote poetry under the pen-name 'Zafar' (Victory).

[2] The double-dome dome is very similar to those of Humayun's tomb, which was built at the same time, and to that of the later Taj Mahal. See Additional Notes, below.

[3] Atgah Khan and Maham Anaga were Akbar's minister and wet-nurse, rather than true foster-parents.

[4] There is a vivid miniature painting of this scene called 'Akbar orders the punishment of his foster-brother' (see Geeti Sen, *Paintings from the Akbar-Nama*, plate 25).

V. The Chausath Khamba[1]

This is a marble hall with sixty-four pillars. It stands a little way off quite near the Mathura road. It is the tomb of Mirza Aziz Kokaltash, the son of Atgah Khan, and it is so beautiful that you should go and see it.

ADDITIONAL NOTES

When you go to Nizamuddin visit the places mentioned, and then try to read for yourself the inscriptions on the buildings. Besides those mentioned there are many others which have inscriptions which you can read for yourself.[2]

The Shrine itself is an epitome of architectural style. The arches were built by Shahjahan. The little arches and pinnacles above are late Mughal, and the dome was built in the nineteenth century. Notice how the work gets poorer stage by stage. The mosque close to the tomb is called the Jama'at Khana Mosque. It is a fine example of the Khilji style. Notice the low flat or half dome, and compare this with the full or semi-circular dome of Atgah Khan's tomb. Atgah Khan's tomb is an excellent example of the early Mughal style. It was probably built by Akbar himself at about the same time as his mother built Humayun's tomb.

If you have the time, you can go to the village of Nizamuddin, where is the tomb of Khan-e-Jahan, the great minister of Firoz Shah Tughlaq, and also a mosque which he built.[3]

Reference: Amir Khusrau, by Mohd Habib. *A Guide to Nizamuddin,* by Maulvi Zafar Hasan (Archaeological Dept Memoirs).

---

[1] Chausath Khamba means sixty-four pillars.

[2] The inscriptions are in Persian.

[3] Khan-e-Jahan's tomb is the first in the octagonal style later used by most of the Lodis and Sayyids. See p. 44 for more on this style. The mosque is Masjid Kalan, not to be confused with the Kalan Masjid near Turkman Gate, which was also built by him. See p. 8, note 4 for more on Khan-e-Jahan.

9. THE LODI TOMBS

The Lodi Tombs stand near Safdarjang's tomb.[1] They are now in the Willingdon Park[2] in New Delhi, and are close to Prithviraj Road. The best way to reach them is by bus to Safdarjang from the Ajmer Gate, or by tonga from the Delhi Gate along the Hardinge Avenue[3] and Prithviraj Road. A turning to the left called South End Road leads you to the main gate of the park in Ratendone Road.[4]

If you enter the Willingdon Park by the main entrance in Ratendone Road you come first to the tomb of Sikandar Shah Lodi. This tomb stands inside a large walled enclosure, and it has recently been repaired by the Government.[5] Sikandar Lodi was the second of the Lodi kings and under him the empire of Delhi recovered some of its former glory. He lived mostly at Agra and built a city there which he called Sikandarabad. Nowadays it is a village which is famous because Akbar's tomb was built there.

The next building you come to is a mosque. Close to the mosque is a great square building with a big dome which looks like a tomb. But it is really the gateway to the mosque. Because it is so large it is called the *Bara Gumbad*. It was built by Abu Amjad, a Mughal noble

[1] See p. 47 and pp. 105–6 for more on the Lodi style.

[2] The Lady Willingdon Park was formed in 1936 on the site of the village of Khairpur; the villagers were given other sites, in nearby Kotla Mubarakpur and in Punjab. Though the old name can still be seen on the northern gate, the name was changed after Independence to Lodi Garden (in the singular, though popularly known as Lodi Gardens). In the 1950s the gardens were re-landscaped by a Japanese team. The greenhouse was added by Joseph Stein who, with Garrett Eckbo, prepared a master plan for Lodi Gardens in 1968. Stein, an American architect who lives in Delhi, also designed the adjoining India International Centre and Ford Foundation offices (see S. White).

[3] Hardinge Avenue is now called Tilak Marg.

[4] This is another symptom of the epidemic of 'Willingdonitis', which spread rapidly in 1930s Delhi (Park, Crescent, Airport, Stadium and Hospital). Ratendone was the courtesy title of Lady Willingdon's son, who in due course became the second Marquis but, apart from having this road named after him thanks to his mother's energetic social engineering, he is otherwise unknown to history. Ratendone Road is now called Amrita Sher-gill Marg, after the acclaimed Indo-Hungarian artist (1913–41). Brassey Avenue, north of Rashtrapati Bhavan, was named for Lady Willingdon's grandfather.

[5] Sikander Lodi's tomb was the precursor of the Mughal garden tombs, beginning with Humayun's.

in the service of Sikandar Lodi (in 1494). Look at the gateway from a distance and see what fine proportions it has. It is the first example in Delhi of what is called the *full* dome, that is, a dome which is a complete semicircle. Near the Bara Gumbad is another tomb very much like the tomb of Sikandar. Some people called this the tomb of Bahlol Lodi.[1] But as it has no inscription we do not know for certain. Probably it is the tomb of one of Sikandar's nobles. In Chiragh Delhi is a tomb which scholars believe to be the tomb of Bahlol Lodi.[2]

Some distance away, near the road which runs from Nizamuddin to Safdarjang, is another tomb. It is like Sikandar Lodi's tomb and is the tomb of Mubarak Shah Sayyid. He was the first of the Sayyid kings and his tomb is the oldest of the Lodi tombs.[3]

Now all these tombs are very much alike. They form a separate style of their own. Some people call this the Pathan style, but the best name for it is the Lodi style, for the Lodis were not frontier Pathans, but Afghans.[4] This style grew up in the fifteenth century after the invasion of Timur, and it lasted until the time of the Mughals.

Here are a few things to notice about these buildings. They will enable you to distinguish them from the buildings of the Mughals and the earlier kings.

Tombs. You will see that the tombs are not square. They are octagonal (eight-sided). Around the tombs are verandahs which are supported by strong square stone pillars. The domes are low or half domes. Around the domes are a number of little *chhattris*. Each chhattri has a little dome, so that the little domes gather round the big ones like chicks round a hen.[5]

---

[1] This is *not* Bahlol Lodi's tomb.

[2] Now confirmed as Bahlol Lodi's tomb.

[3] The road referred to is Lodi Road. This tomb is actually that of Muhammed Shah Sayyid, the nephew and successor of Mubarak Shah, whose tomb is in the village of Kotla Mubarakpur, east of South Extension Part I. The names can be confusing, because Muhammed Shah was known as Mubarak (Fortunate) Khan; the tomb was erected by his son. Spear has slipped up here. Muhammed Shah was the *third* (not first) Sayyid king.

[4] By 'some people' Spear means, for example, Bishop Heber who, writing about 'Pathan' architecture, said that 'they built like giants and finished their work like jewellers'.

[5] There were actually two styles of Sayyid and Lodi tombs. They were either

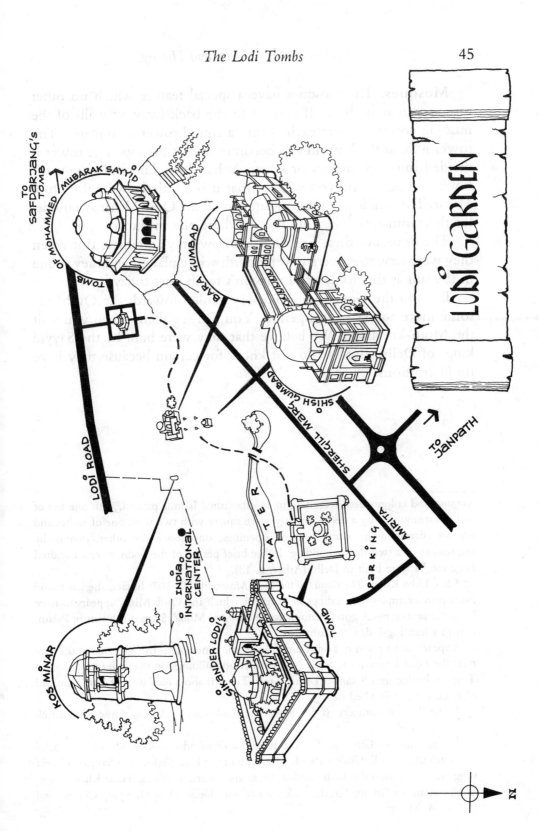

LODI GARDEN

TO JANPATH

TO SAFDARJANG'S TOMB

MUBARAK SAYYID

TOMB OF MOHAMMED

BARA GUMBAD

SHISH GUMBAD

SHERGILL MARG

PARKING

AMRITA

WATER

LODI ROAD

INDIA INTERNATIONAL CENTER

KOS MINAR

SIKANDER LODI'S TOMB

N

Mosques. The mosques have a special feature which no other mosques in India have. If you go to the back (or west wall) of the mosque you will see at each corner a round tower or minaret. The tower is fat at the bottom and becomes thin at the top. The tower is divided into five storeys or stages. What does this remind you of? Look at it again and you will see that it is a little copy of the Qutb Minar. The builders of these mosques used the Qutb Minar as a model for their minarets. They did this nowhere else in India.[1]

The domes of these buildings are now grey and dirty. But when they were new they were covered with white plaster, and they shone in the sun as the dome of Humayun's tomb does today.[2]

Beyond the Government nursery garden towards the Qutb[3] are some more tombs of this period. You can see them when you visit the Moth-ki-Masjid. We believe that they were built by the Sayyid kings of Delhi. But we do not know for certain because they have no inscriptions.[4]

---

octagonal and colonnaded, according to an established Islamic pattern, with one tier of arches surmounted by a dome; or they were square with two tiers, one of arches and one of corresponding sham window openings, one above the other, giving the impression of a two-storey building. In the brief period of the Lodis, over a hundred large tombs were built in Delhi (Asher, p. 13).

[1] See Ebba Koch, *The Copies of the Qutb Minar*, pp. 95–107. In fact, she has found numerous examples of buildings in India for which the Qutb Minar appears to have been the prototype. A good example is the Hashtsal Minar, 5 km northwest of Palam, part of a hunting-lodge of Shahjahan.

[2] Spear's description of Lodi Garden has some omissions – the *kos minar* at the gate near the Ford Foundation, some Mughal-period buildings on the eastern side, and a Tughlaq bridge near Sikander Lodi's tomb. There is also a *baoli* west of Bara Gumbad now unfortunately filled in.

[3] The 'Karbala' nursery garden across the road from Safdarjang Airport has a rich collection of plants.

[4] Bare Khan ka Gumbad, Chhote Khan ka Gumbad and Kale Khan ka Gumbad are north of South Extension Part I. These are of the Lodi period, not Sayyid as Spear suggests. Apart from the Lodi Garden, there are other tombs near Hauz Khas village, Bagh-i-Alam ka Gumbad in the park west of Aurobindo Place Shopping Centre, and in Ramakrishnapuram.

Additional Notes

The Lodi Style. See the special architectural section.[1] In the group of tombs note specially:

(i)   The walled enclosure of Sikandar Lodi's tomb. This was to prevent the tombs from being plundered, and is evidence of the insecurity of the times.

(ii)   The *Bara Gumbad*, which is the finest gateway of the fifteenth century in Delhi. You should stand at a distance in order that you may see its good proportions.

(iii) The tomb of Mubarak Shah Sayyid. This tomb is quite complete and only lacks the original plaster. Remember that much of the ornamentation of the plaster was coloured and you can imagine what the tombs originally looked like.

Both the Lodi and Sayyid tombs are built of stone and plaster. Marble was not used because both dynasties were poor and needed their money for wars.

10. THE MOTH-KI-MASJID

You can visit the Moth-ki-Masjid in the cold weather. It is a long way out of Delhi and for that reason very few people visit it.[2] There are two ways of reaching the Moth-ki-Masjid. Firstly you can take a tonga and drive along the Qutb road and past Safdarjang's tomb and the aerodrome. About a mile further, on the left hand side of the road, is a sign-post to the Moth-ki-Masjid. From this sign-post a *kachha* road leads straight to the masjid, which is in the village of Masjid-Moth. It is about one mile from the main Qutb road.[3] Secondly, you can, if you like, walk from Safdarjang's tomb. If you go this way you take a path across the fields. It leaves the Qutb road near the Aliganj[4]

---

[1] Chapter 22 (pp. 105–6).

[2] This area, between South Extension Part II and Niti Bagh, is in the southern *centre* of 1990s Delhi, and could no longer be described as 'a long way out'.

[3] The Moth-ki-Masjid is south of South Extension Part II, off Aurobindo Marg (formerly Qutb road).

[4] The Aliganj Enclosure was a massive wall, east of the present Aurobindo Marg, enclosing some buildings erected by Qudsia Begum in 1750 (*cf* p. 16). The enclosure and fields have now been built over by the INA Market, Kidwai Nagar and South Extension.

enclosure and just opposite the Willingdon Airport.[1] The country is quite open and you will see a group of large tombs in the distance. These are called the Sayyid tombs[2] and you should walk straight towards them. From these tombs there is a path to Masjid-Moth. The whole distance is about two miles. Moth-ki-Masjid is on one side of the village Masjid-Moth. It was built by Mian Buhwa, the Wazir of Sikandar Shah Lodi. It is said that one day the Wazir went with the king a mosque to pray. Just before prayer a bird dropped a seed of the moth plant, so that the king knelt on it. When he rose up the Wazir saw the moth seed. He picked it up and said to himself, 'A seed so honoured by His Majesty must not be thrown away. It must be used in the service of God.' So he took the moth seed and planted it. The seed that came up he planted again, and he did this again and again. At last he was able to sell the moth for a great sum. He sowed the seed and sold the grain until he had enough money to build a mosque. Then he built the mosque which you now see, and he called it Moth-ki-Masjid in honour of the grain of the moth which Sikandar Shah had knelt upon.

The Moth-ki-Masjid is one of the two most beautiful mosques in Delhi built between the invasion of Timur and the coming of the Mughals. The other one is in the Purana Qila and is called Sher Shah's mosque.

You enter the mosque from the village street by a very beautiful gateway. Notice the different colours of the stones in the gateway, red, blue, black and white. They make a beautiful pattern. Then look

---

[1] A Flying Club was set up at Palam in 1929 and then moved here. Lord Willingdon was the first Viceroy to have a personal plane. The airport was the headquarters of the South East Command Air Wing during World War II; later it played an important role in ferrying refugees to India after Partition in 1947. It was renamed Safdarjang Airport after Independence. Until the flyover was built in 1966, this was known as 'Murder Mile' because of the dangerous conjuncture of road, railway line and flight path.

When the airport was established, the dome of Safdarjang's Tomb was lit as a warning to low-flying aircraft. At night the dome of the tomb was suffused with a soft red glow which, in the relatively subdued lighting of the city in those days, could be seen from some distance away. Nowadays Delhi suffers from the same 'light pollution' as other major cities of the world, and casual star-gazing by city-dwellers is less and less rewarding as a result.

[2] See p. 46, note 4.

at the arch carefully. You will see that there
is a Hindu arch like Fig. 3, inside a Muslim
arch like Fig 4. so the whole arch looks like
Fig. 5. This shows that Hindus as well as
Muslims helped to build this mosque. It
shows how Hindus and Muslims worked
together in Delhi in those days to build
beautiful buildings to the glory of God.

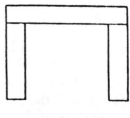

FIG. 3

FIG. 4   FIG. 5

From the roof of the mosque you have a fine view of all the
Delhis.[1] On one side is the Qutb Minar, Siri, the Bijay Mandal and
Chiragh Delhi. On the horizon you can see the walls of Tughlaqabad.
Look from the mosque roof over the village and you will see
Humayun's tomb, the Purana Qila and the Khan-e-Khanan's tomb.[2]
Look again towards New Delhi and you will see Safdarjang's tomb,
the Lodi tombs and the Jama Masjid in the distance. In no other city
can you see so many historical monuments in one place.

As you return to Safdarjang's tomb you will see that the whole
plain shows signs of ruins of all sorts. The reason for this is that from
the time of Firoz Shah to the time of Shahjahan the city of Delhi was
centred round, first Firoz Shah's Kotla and then round the Purana
Qila. This land was on the outskirts of the city, and so it was a
convenient place for nobles and kings to build their tombs and
gardens.

[1] Sadly visitors are no longer allowed to climb the mosque and, even if you could,
you would no longer be able to see 'all the Delhis'. There are very few monuments
which are still accessible in the way Spear describes.

[2] See p. 108, note 1.

11. SAFDARJANG'S TOMB

Today we shall take a tonga and drive to Safdarjang's tomb. Safdarjang's tomb is the last of the great Mughal tombs. It is as large as Humayun's tomb,[1] but it is not so beautiful. Have you ever thought of the reason? There are two reasons. The first reason is that the materials used are not so good as in Humayun's tomb. Instead of a rich red stone the builders used a light brown stone which looks like a flower which has faded.[2] Look at the dome and you will see that the marble has dirty yellow patches. That is because the marble is not so good as that of Humayun's tomb. The builders of those days used these materials because they were poor and could not afford the best stone or marble. The second reason that the tomb is not so beautiful as Humayun's is that the shape is not so good. The builders of those days were not so skilful as in the time of Humayun.[3] Very few people could afford fine buildings in those days and so the builders had less practice in building. Safdarjang was the last of the great Mughal nobles who built a great tomb. He was the second Nawab of Oudh, and succeeded his uncle Saadat Khan in 1739. Saadat Ali took poison when Nadir Shah took Delhi and insulted him there. For several years Safdarjang was Wazir of the empire. He was dismissed by Ahmad Shah in favour of Ghaziuddin, Imadulmulk, in 1752. For six months Safdarjang and Imadulmulk waged a civil war in Delhi. Imadulmulk with the Emperor Ahmad Shah held Shahjahanabad. Safdarjang held the Purana Qila and Firozabad and all the suburbs which lay between them. In those days these suburbs were called 'Old Delhi' and Shahjahanabad was 'New Delhi'. Safdarjang was not a good soldier. At last he was defeated and returned to his *subah* of Oudh.[4] His son

---

[1] Safdarjang's tomb *is* large, but its podium (110 feet square) is nevertheless much smaller than that of Humayun's (370 feet square). 'The last of the Mughal tombs' is misleading, since Safdarjang was *not* a Mughal.

[2] Bishop Heber, writing in the 1820s, called it 'the colour of potted meat'. The marble used for the building is said to have been removed from the mausoleum of Abdur Rahim Khan-e-Khanan.

[3] See p. 53 and pp. 107–9 for more on Late Mughal architectural style.

[4] Nawab Saadat Khan, Governor of Awadh (Oudh), was one of the Mughal army commanders defeated by the Persian ruler Nadir Shah at the Battle of Panipat; he subsequently committed suicide. His nephew Safdarjang succeeded him in Awadh and

Shuja-ud-Daula fought against the English and made a treaty with Clive. He was the founder of the state of Oudh, which was annexed by Dalhousie.[1] The Nawabs of Oudh maintained the tomb until the Mutiny and it was one of the sights of Delhi. On each of three sides of the garden you will see pavilions. These were used by the Nawab's family when they came to Delhi on visits.

Now Safdarjang's tomb is again important because it is a landmark for aeroplanes coming to Delhi. Every night the dome is lit up by a red light, so that the aeroplanes can see the right place to land in safety.

A little way along the Qutb road, on the left-hand side of the road, you will see a low stone platform. This is the tomb of Mirza Najaf Khan.[2] For ten years he was the chief minister of Shah Alam (1772–82). He was a great soldier and statesman and restored to Delhi some of its former glory. At his death he had 60,000 troops under his own command. Shah Alam found no worthy successor to Mirza Najaf Khan, and soon after fell under the dominion of the Maratha, Madhav Rao Sindhia. The town of Najafgarh was the centre of his jagir[3] and is named after him. The police station there is his old mansion. After his death Shah Alam's kingdom became so small that men repeated the rhyme

Az Delhi to Palam
Badshahi Shah Alam.

---

became concurrently Wazir at Delhi. Ghaziuddin Imadulmulk prevailed on the weak emperor Ahmad Shah to dismiss Safdarjang as Wazir, a post which Ghaziuddin wanted for himself. The defeated Safdarjang retired to Awadh and died soon after.

[1] Under Safdarjang, his son Shujauddaula and their successors, Awadh became virtually independent of the Mughal emperor, and rivalled Delhi in literature, music, painting and architecture (as Satyajit Ray depicted in 'Shatranj Ke Khilari' – 'The Chess Players'). This golden age of elegance and civilized living was given a severe jolt in 1856 with the annexation of Awadh. As *Punch* of 22 March 1856 put it:

"*'Peccavi, I've Scinde' wrote Lord Ellen so proud.*

More briefly Dalhousie wrote – '*Vovi, I've Oude.*' " (In Latin, *Peccavi* = I've sinned; *Vovi* = I've vowed). The spell was finally shattered with the events of 1857.

[2] This, like the tomb of Dariya Khan further south in Kidwai Nagar, is unusual in being *open*; the grave is in the centre of a large platform, set in a garden.

[3] Jagir's literal meaning is place, but it is used to refer to the landholdings given on lease as a favour from the emperor. Najafgarh is due east of Palam.

From Delhi to Palam
Is the realm of Shah Alam[1]

Now we will walk to the Willingdon Airport. You see that all
around you is a great plain. This is the place where a great battle was
fought between Timur and the Emperor of Delhi, Mohammed Tughlaq[2] and his general Mallu Khan. Just like Nadir Shah, Timur marched
to Delhi without opposition because the Delhi nobles were quarrell-
ing amongst themselves. Disunity has always meant disaster for India.
Timur encamped near Loni (near Shahdara) with 100,000 captives.
He crossed the Jumna near Metcalfe House and rode to the Ridge.
There Mohammed attacked him, but was repulsed. The prisoners
were so pleased when they heard the battle that on his return Timur
ordered them all to be executed. After this Timur crossed with his
whole army. He marched along the Ridge and over the present city
until he reached the aerodrome. Mohammed Tughlaq collected his
army from Jahanpanah (near Mehrauli) and marched out to meet him.
Mohammed had many elephants whom the Mongols feared, but
Timur had very good horsemen. The Mongols charged the Indian
cavalry and defeated them. Then the elephants ran back on their own
men and completed the defeat. The Indian army fought bravely but
Timur was too strong for them. Timur stayed a fortnight in Delhi.
Then he crossed the Jumna at the ford by the railway bridge,[3] and
marched to Meerut. Timur chose this place for the battle because it
was flat and open. There were no hills or houses and so the Mongol
cavalry could easily charge.

---

[1] There is a play on words here: 'Shah Alam' means 'Emperor of the World'. After
the death of Shah Alam in 1806, in the twilight of Mughal Delhi, 'there [was] left the
glitter and culture of the nobles without their suicidal struggle for power, the dignity
and learning of the court without its folly and its weakness. Literary style replaced
political . . . and successive literary emperors presided over a mild literary and intellec-
tual renaissance' (Spear, *A Historical Sketch*, p. 79). It has been suggested that the poem's
Shah Alam is not the Mughal but the last Sayyid king, Alauddin Alam Shah (Abdul
Haleem, *History of the Lodi Sultans*, p. 12).

[2] *Mahmud* Tughlaq, actually.

[3] Spear is here again visualizing all the events associated with one site as if they
were happening simultaneously; obviously neither Metcalfe House, nor the aerodrome,
nor the railway bridge yet existed!

ADDITIONAL NOTES

1. **Safdarjang's tomb**. For the special features of the late Mughal style, see the architectural section.[1]

Notice the poorness of the materials used in the buildings. Notice also how the garden with its pavilions was used as a residence after Safdarjang himself died. The tomb itself was only used as a residence during the lifetime of the founder. The rooms round the tomb were used for entertainment afterwards, but not for residence. That is why the side pavilions were built.[2]

2. *Mirza Najaf Khan*. You will find an account of this man in H.G. Keene's *Fall of the Mughal Empire* or Francklin's *History of the Reign of Shah Alam*. The latter is the best but it is very old. There is a copy in the Hardinge Library. There is also Syed Ghulam Hussain's *Seir-ul-Mutaqherin*. There is an English translation which ought to be in your library. It is also in the Hardinge Library. Najaf Khan was a great man, though he is almost forgotten today.

3. You can trace for yourselves, on a map of Delhi district, Timur's movements before the battle with Mohammed Tughlaq. Remember that the Mongols of Timur were very different from the Mughals of Babur. The Mongols of Chinghiz Khan and of Timur were very fierce and slew all who crossed their path, Hindu or Muslim. Remember what Amir Khusrau says about them. But Babur was a highly cultured man and so were most of his nobles. They had been refined by a hundred years of Persian culture.[3]

---

[1] See pp. 107–8 for more on the architecture of Mughal tombs.

[2] Safdarjang did not build his own mausoleum, though he may well have indicated his wish to be buried here rather than in Faizabad, then the capital of Awadh. The tomb was built by his son Shujauddaula. The complex also housed a *madarsa* and even today is known as 'Safdarjang Madarsa', and not 'Safdarjang Maqbara' (Tomb). The pavilions had the evocative names of Jangli Mahal (Forest Palace) to the west, Moti Mahal (Pearl Palace) to the north, and Badshah Pasand (The King's Favourite) to the south. Badshah Pasand is now occupied by the ASI, which also maintains a library in the beautiful tomb gateway.

[3] Amir Khusrau's description is on p. 70, note 1. The word 'Mongol' is used for the nomadic Central Asians, who under Chinghiz Khan (universal sovereign) created the 'largest contiguous land empire in human history' (Embree, vol iii, p. 23). Despite repeated raids, they failed to conquer north India. In the fourteenth century the people of the western Mongol empire became settled, after conversion to Islam; in the sixteenth century the people of the eastern part became Buddhist. Babur and his successors, whose ancestry was Turko-Mongol, and belonged to the urban culture of Samarkand, are known as Mughals (the Persian word for Mongol).

Part III

THE QUTB DISTRICT

12. THE GREAT MOSQUE

(Quwwat-ul-Islam Masjid)

There are so many interesting things to see at Mehrauli, that you must make up your mind to visit them *one by one*. If you run about from one building to another you will not remember much about any of the buildings. Think of a marriage feast. If you run about from room to room and court to court instead of sitting down in the right place, you will not get anything to eat. In the same way if you run from building to building you will not take anything away with you. Today we will visit first the great mosque close to the Qutb Minar, called the **Quwwat-ul-Islam** mosque.

We will go first to the dak bungalow close to the Qutb Minar. From the dak bungalow you go up some steps into the great enclosure of the mosque.[1] The mosque is in three parts and we will go straight along the path which leads to the gateway of the oldest portion. Now we are inside, in a courtyard of stone pillars. In front of us is the Iron Pillar, and just beyond, the ruins of three great arches.

This mosque was begun by Qutbuddin Aibak in 1191 A.D. Qutbuddin had no masons with him, so he made the Hindu masons of Prithviraj's Lal Kot[2] build the mosque for him. He took the square stone pillars which you see round the court from some Hindu temples. But at the western end of the mosque he wanted pointed arches, like the mosques of Ghor in Afghanistan.[3] But the Hindu workmen did not know about pointed arches and keystones. (The note on architecture at the end of this book explains what a keystone is.)[4] So they

---

[1] The dak bungalow is on the left, just inside the entrance to the Qutb complex, but there is a tall hedge between it and the public footpath, discouraging casual visitors. It is used by the Delhi Administration.

[2] See Section 14 below.

[3] See p. 57 and pp. 102–3 on the introduction of the pointed arch to India.

[4] Chapter 22.

built arches without keystones. Arches which have no keystones are very weak and will not carry any weight. Next they had to decorate the arches. The Hindu workmen wanted to carve beautiful figures, but the king would not allow this. The king wanted texts from the Koran in Arabic, but the workmen did not know much about these. So in the end they carved a beautiful plant growing up the arch and put Arabic texts in between the leaves.

In the centre of the courtyard is the Iron Pillar. This was erected by a Hindu king called Chandra about 400 A.D. It has an inscription which tells of his victories. This pillar is famous because it is of almost pure iron. It is very difficult to make bars of pure iron, and so this pillar proves that the Hindu workmen were skilful in working metals.

This mosque was the Jama Masjid of the Sultans of Delhi for thirty years. Then Sultan Iltutmish decided that he would make it bigger. So he built six more great arches, three on each side of the first mosque. Some of these arches are still complete. By this time workmen had come from Ghor and Persia, and they brought their own knowledge with them. So you will find that the carving on Iltutmish's arches is quite different from that on Qutbuddin's arches. Instead of flowers and plants there are little circles and triangles and other shapes. This is called geometrical design because it is like the figures you study in geometry.

Iltutmish built his own tomb at one corner of his new mosque. It is of red stone and is covered with carving just like the carving on the arches of his mosque.[1]

Iltutmish's mosque was the Jama Masjid of Delhi for nearly a hundred years. Then Alauddin Khilji, who had conquered the south of India and brought its treasure back to Delhi, decided to build a still bigger mosque. He began to build six more great arches, starting from the tomb of Iltutmish. He built the beautiful gateway close to the Qutb Minar and he meant to build two more like it. This gateway is called the **Alai Darwaza** after him. It has the same sort of carving as Iltutmish's tomb, and it is the finest gateway at Mehrauli. But before Alauddin had finished this mosque he died, and his son never troubled to complete it. Firoz Shah built a new Jama Masjid in the city of Firozabad in 1360. Timur visited the Qutb mosque when he took Delhi in 1398 and after this time the great mosque fell into decay

[1] See p. 57 for more on Iltutmish's tomb.

along with the old city of Delhi. Thus it remained until Lord Dalhousie ordered the repair of the arches at the request of Sir Thomas Metcalfe's daughter.[1] In 1904 Lord Curzon visited the Qutb. He founded the Archaeological Department which now carefully preserves all that is left of this great mosque.[2]

Just behind the arches of Qutbuddin and Iltutmish and near the Minar are some more buildings. They were built by Alauddin as a madarsa or college. You can still trace the rooms in which the students used to live while they learnt Arabic and studied the Koran. It is probable that Alauddin was himself buried there.

ADDITIONAL NOTES

The temple pillars which were used in Qutbuddin's mosque belonged to the style known as the Jain style of Rajputana and Gujarat. The best examples of this style are the marble Jain temples at Mount Abu.[3] Qutbuddin built a mosque at Ajmer in just the same way as he did at Delhi. It is called the **Arhai-din-ki-Jhompra**, because it is said to have been built in two-and-a-half days.[4]

When you visit the Qutb mosque, first examine the carving done by Hindu workmen on the arches of Qutbuddin's mosque, and then look at Iltutmish's arches and tomb. Then you will easily see the difference between the two styles. The former is called 'naturalistic' because it imitates nature

---

[1] Earl (later Marquis) Dalhousie was Governor General during 1848–56. Emily Metcalfe's Reminiscences have been edited by M.M. Kaye and included in *The Golden Calm*.

[2] The Archaeological Survey of India was founded in 1861; Curzon improved the working of the provincial Surveys and appointed the great archaeologist, Sir John Marshall, as Director-General. Through the Ancient Monuments Act (1904), the government was given wide powers to 'protect' monuments including the erection of the warning blue signboards at all listed sites. Curzon took an indefatigable personal interest in India's architectural heritage: 'As a pilgrim at the shrine of beauty, I have visited them, but as a priest in the temple of duty have I charged myself with their reverent custody and their studious repair' (Fraser, *India Under Curzon and After*, p. 359).

[3] 'Rajputana' was the term used before Independence for the area roughly covered by present-day Rajasthan. The reference is to the Jain Dilwara temples in Mount Abu.

[4] Arhai-din-ki-Jhompra (literally two-and-a-half days' hut). This was built by Qutbuddin, with additions by Iltutmish.

and follows its lines and curves; the latter is called 'geometrical' or 'formal', because it consists of straight lines and circles like those used in geometry.

The use of the arch in Delhi buildings and the importance of the keystone are explained in the architectural section. You should read this section before visiting the Qutb. Draw the diagrams given there for yourself, and then you will understand the points mentioned very easily.

You will notice that the tomb of Iltutmish has no roof. Experts believe that it never had a dome. It seems strange that such a tomb should have no covering; perhaps it had a plain roof made of beams of timber.[1] Iltutmish's tomb is one of the oldest Muslim tombs in India. The oldest known tomb is that of his eldest son Nasiruddin Mohammed, who died before him in 1228–9. It is about two miles from Mehrauli, and makes a good walk in the cold weather. It is called locally the tomb of Sultan Ghari.[2] The garden close to the dak bungalow was built in the eighteenth century and is a good example of a late Mughal pleasure garden.[3]

The two Minars are dealt with in a separate chapter.

13. THE QUTB MINAR[4]

When you look up at the Qutb Minar, there is a question which you will ask at once. What was the reason for building it? Was it just a monument built by a king to please himself or was it built for a special purpose? Some people think it was meant to be a minaret for giving the call to prayer. But see how tall it is. A man standing on the top can hardly be heard below. Then look at the position of the Minar. It is not joined on either side to Qutbuddin's mosque, or to Iltutmish's mosque. We do not know for certain what its purpose was, but it

---

[1] This may seem to us lacking in appropriate pomp for an emperor, but it appears to be a tradition for devout Muslims (see, for example, what Spear says about Jahanara's grave on p. 39.) 'Tombs are sometimes left uncovered, even when inside a mausoleum . . . the motive was the conviction that a grave not exposed to the rain and the dew was unblessed' (James Dickie in Michell, p. 45).

[2] Sultan Ghari's tomb is now surrounded by the buildings of Vasant Kunj's C Block.

[3] The 'Mughal pleasure garden' is to the right of the path leading towards the Qutb, and is entered by a small gateway.

[4] The word 'Qutb' means axis/pole, so Qutb Minar means 'axial tower' and Qutbuddin 'staff of God'. There is another Qutbuddin at Mehrauli: the Persian saint Khwaja Qutbuddin Bakhtiyar Kaki (d.1235), whose shrine is described on p. 64. The name Mehrauli is thought to be derived from Mehrewali, meaning 'blessings of the saint', i.e. Khwaja Qutbuddin.

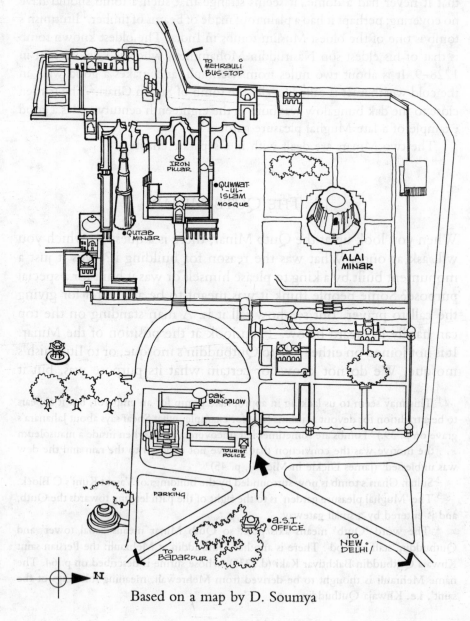

Based on a map by D. Soumya

was probably built as a Tower of Victory. There are towers of victory something like it at Ghazni and Ghor. We know that kings built towers to celebrate their victories. Probably Qutbuddin started the Minar to celebrate his victory.[1]

The Qutb Minar is one of the most famous towers in the world. It is 234 feet high and the highest single tower in the world. The other famous towers are the Leaning Tower of Pisa (in Italy) and the Great Pagoda in Pekin (China), but they are not so high as the Qutb Minar.

Some people think that the Minar was commenced by Prithviraj or his uncle Vigraharaja who conquered Delhi from the Tomar Rajputs.[2] We do not know for certain, but if either of them started it, Qutbuddin and Iltutmish finished it. The Minar was finished about 1200 A.D. and it has stood, like a sentinel on watch over Delhi, ever since. When Alauddin returned from his wars in the Deccan he thought he would build another Tower of Victory to celebrate his victories. It was to be twice as high as the Qutb Minar. You can see the ruins of this great tower on the other side of the Qutbuddin's mosque. But Alauddin died when it was only just begun, and no one has ever finished it.

In the reign of Firoz Shah an earthquake damaged the two top storeys. Firoz Shah repaired the Minar and added a little pavilion at the top. It was repaired again by Sikandar Lodi in 1505. Later, in 1794, the Minar was damaged again. Major Smith, an engineer, repaired it, and instead of Firoz Shah's pavilion he placed a pavilion of his own on the top. In 1848 Lord Hardinge removed this and it now stands in the garden between the dak bungalow and the Minar.[3] You can see the two storeys which Firoz Shah built because they are built of white marble and are quite smooth.[4] The lower three storeys

[1] The reference is to the ruined minar at Siyah Push, near Ghazni, the minaret of Bahram Shah at Ghazni and that of Jham (near Herat), all built in the twelfth century. (There are of course also towers of victory outside the Islamic world, such as Nelson's Column, for example.)

[2] See first paragraph of Additional Notes on p. 61.

[3] See second paragraph of Additional Notes on p. 61. The stone cupola was damaged by another earthquake in 1794. Major Smith's cupola – of late Mughal design – was fixed in 1803 (see Spear, *A Historical Sketch*, p. 32). The cupola is still in the grounds, near Imam-i-Zamin's tomb, and looks as good as new!

[4] Spear is contrasting the smooth surface of the marble, not just with the relatively rough surface of the sandstone but with the alternating ridges and curves of its carving.

are the ones which Qutbuddin and Iltutmish built. They are built of red stone and have ribs of stone which run up the Minar.

If you look at the Qutb Minar very carefully from a distance you will see that the Minar is not quite perpendicular, that is, it leans a little to one side. That is the result of the various earthquakes which have shaken it. Nowadays it is very carefully looked after by the Archaeological Department, and they fill up any cracks in the walls as soon as they appear.[1]

Now let us look at the Minar more closely. In the lower storeys there is beautiful carving like that on the tomb of Iltutmish. Round the tower are inscriptions. These record that Iltutmish completed the tower. The walls are sloping in order to make the tower stronger. If you jumped from the top you would never reach the ground. You would hit the side of the Minar because the walls slope outwards so much. Even if you were a very good jumper you would do this.

We will mount the stairs to the top.[2] Count them as you go up and see if you get the right total. There are 378. From the top of the Minar there is the finest view of all the Delhis. Look just below and trace out the walls of Lal Kot. Look along the road to Delhi and you will see on the left hand the Hauz Khas and on the right hand the walls of Jahanpanah and Siri. From here the Khilji and Tughlaq kings watched the wild Mongol hordes when they threatened Delhi. From here Mohammed Tughlaq watched Timur's army camped on the Willingdon Airport. Further off you will see on one side the walls of Tughlaqabad. On another side you see Humayun's Tomb and the Purana Qila. Then come Firoz Shah Kotla and the domes of the Jama Masjid.

On another side is Safdarjang's tomb and New Delhi. On the last side is the rocky ground to the south west. On this side is the tomb of Sultan Ghari among the rocks. Notice how the roads are marked by the avenues of trees. When the land is dry they look like green snakes wriggling across the country. Except for Rome, there is no finer view of historical buildings in the world.

---

[1] The Minar is 2 feet off the perpendicular. See also third paragraph of Additional Notes (p. 61).

[2] Visitors are no longer allowed to climb the Qutb Minar. (Until 1981 one could climb the first 90′ to the first storey, but after an accident that too was banned.)

ADDITIONAL NOTES

There is a learned controversy as to the origin of the Minar. The case for the Hindu origin of the Minar is given by Rai Bahadur Kanwar Sain in an article in the *Punjab University Historical Society Journal*, Vol. III, Part II, No. 6 (December 1934). Rai Bahadur Sain thinks it was started by Vigraha-raja, Prithviraj's uncle and predecessor. In any case it was finished by Qutbuddin and Iltutmish. [1]

The chhattri which Major Smith placed on the top of the Minar was removed by Lord Hardinge in 1848 because its style was quite different from that of the rest of the Minar. Note that this Lord Hardinge was the Governor-General of 1844–8 and not the recent Viceroy from 1910 to 1916.

If you look at the bottom of the Minar carefully, you will see a number of little glass plates held in position by concrete bands. These glass plates have been put there by the Archaeological Department. If there is the slightest movement of the Minar, or the smallest crack in the stone, the glass will break. You will very likely see one or two of them cracked. The engineers then fill up the cracks with liquid cement, and so keep the Minar strong and safe. At the time of the Bihar earthquake a number of these glasses cracked. A very careful watch is kept on the Minar by the engineers. [2] The Archaeological Department have published an excellent handbook on the Qutb Minar and Mosque. You should read this in your school library.

14. THE LAL KOT (MEHRAULI)

We will spend today visiting some of the other interesting places at Mehrauli. Remember that Mehrauli was the capital of the Indian Empire for two centuries and during that time it was one of the largest cities in the world. [3] So do not think that when you have seen the Mosque and the Minar you have seen the whole city!

---

[1] No scholar today seriously suggests that the Minar is of older origin than the Turkish rulers. We know that Hindu masons were employed to build the minar because they left behind the equivalent of 'Kilroy was here' messages – beloved by builders the world over – in the form of carved graffiti in Devnagiri, the script used for Hindi (see M.C. Joshi *Some Nagari Inscriptions on the Qutb Minar*, pp. 3–7).

[2] Two of these glass plates ('tell-tales') can be seen on the first storey on the same side as the entrance. The Bihar earthquake referred to was in 1934.

[3] Mehrauli, along the Delhi Ridge, was a town in the kingdoms of both the Tomars and the Chauhans (Chahamanas), Rajput dynasties. The 'two centuries' Spear refers

When you drive to Mehrauli you will notice that you go up a hill just before you arrive. Nearly at the top of this hill you will see some earth and stones dug out on either side of the road. We will stop the bus and get down to look at it. You will see that these stones are part of a wall. This wall is a piece of the city wall of the Hindu city of Delhi. The archaeologists have recently excavated it, so that we can see what it is like.[1] You will notice that the wall is very thick and strong. The archaeologists have only excavated a small portion of the wall. But a mound of earth covers the rest of it. If you stand on the Qutb Minar you can trace the whole circuit of the wall and see just how big the old city of Delhi was. You will see that it was not very large.

Now we come to the entrance of the Qutb Mosque. Here the road forks. The right hand fork goes to Mehrauli town: the left hand to Tughlaqabad. We will take the left fork first. Just past the dak bungalow you will see an old tomb. This is interesting because it was once used by Sir Thomas Metcalfe.[2] He used to come here during the rains as a change from his great house at Delhi. Half a mile further we come to a mound by the side of the road with a notice saying that it is the Badayun Gate. In the days of the Sultans, Badayun was a great city, and this was the gate that people who wanted to go there passed through.[3] You can imagine a great concourse of people here. Camels and mules brought merchandise, soldiers on horseback pushed through the crowd, noblemen on elephants and their ladies in palanquins went by in stately procession. Their servants cleared the way

---

to was the high period of the Delhi Sultanate, 1192–1398, during which Mehrauli remained a lively settlement, although the centre of the dynasty moved northwards as far as Firozabad on the River Yamuna. Unlike some of the later Delhis, it has been continuously inhabited and built on ever since.

[1] The remains of the walls of Qila Rai Pithora ('Fort of Raja Prithviraj Chauhan') can also be seen elsewhere in Mehrauli and Saket; this is now the intersection of the Saket Road and Aurobindo Marg.

[2] The tomb is of Mohammad Quli Khan, the brother of Adham Khan, who is commemorated by the spectacular tomb nearby (see next page). Sir Thomas Metcalfe (1795–1853) adopted this '*tombe ornée*' as a weekend retreat which he called Dilkusha, or 'Heart's Desire'. This now rather dilapidated structure, whitened by *chunam*, is on a low hill, outside the landscaped Qutb complex. He compiled 'The Delhie Book' in 1844, which was published as *The Golden Calm*, ed. M. Kaye, pp. 201 onwards.

[3] Badayun, a centre of Islamic learning as early as the twelfth century, is a town about 200 km south-east of Delhi; Badayun Gate, east of the Qutb, is now in ruins.

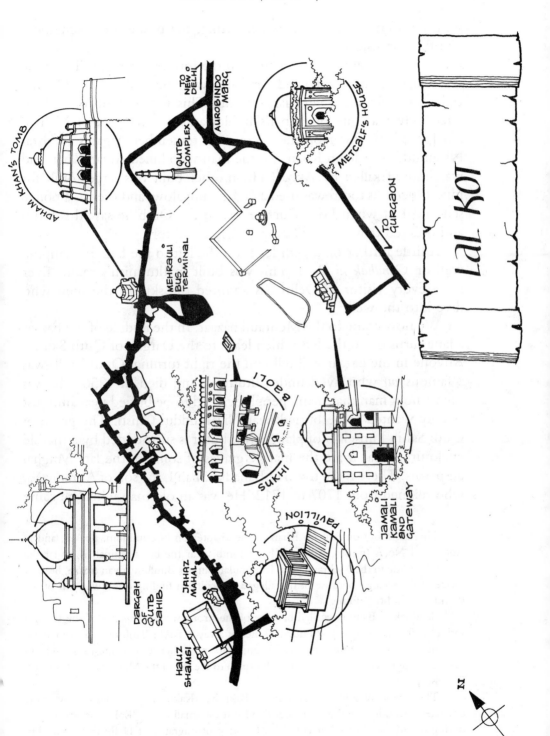

with loud cries. Great was the shouting, the bustle, the excitement and the confusion.

Now we will retrace our steps to the fork of the roads. This time we will take the right-hand fork and walk into Mehrauli. On the right you will see a very large tomb. This is the tomb of Adham Khan. He was one of Akbar's nobles and was the son of Maham Anaga and his foster-brother. You will remember Atgah's tomb at Nizamuddin. Adham Khan was the man who killed Atgah Khan and was himself killed by Akbar. His mother built this large tomb for him. Once this tomb was used as a dak bungalow, and then as a police station.[1] But when Lord Curzon visited the Qutb he saw this tomb and ordered that it should be properly cared for.

A little further on a path leads off the left to the famous jumping well or *Gandhak ki Baoli*. This was built in Iltutmish's reign. Ever since every visitor to Delhi has admired the skill of the men who dive into the well.[2]

We now come to the Mehrauli bazaar. In the middle of the bazaar a lane turns off to the left which leads to the Dargah of Qutb Sahib.[3] Anyone in the bazaar will tell you the right turning. Qutb Sahib was a famous *pir* who lived under Iltutmish and died in 1236. He was such a holy man that many people wanted to be buried near him just as they wanted to be buried near Nizamuddin Chisti. The grave of Qutb Sahib himself is of plain earth, but it is surrounded by a marble enclosure. Near it are the marble graves of some of the late Mughal emperors. There is the tomb of Bahadur Shah I, the son of Aurangzeb, who reigned from 1707 to 1712. He was an old man when he came

[1] There is more on Adham Khan in the chapter on Nizamuddin, pp. 41, and in Additional Notes (p. 66). Adham Khan's tomb, near the bus terminal, is by far the largest building in the Mehrauli area. Its popular name is Bhulbhulaiyan (maze, literally 'place of forgetting') because of the alleged difficulty of finding one's way out of the corridor round the dome.

[2] Gandhak ki Baoli (so called because of the strong smell – *gandh* – of the sulphur spring) is five storeys deep. About 100 metres away is Sukhi Baoli or Rajon-ki-Bain. This dramatic three-storey step well is quite dry now, hence its name (Sukhi means dry). The approach is still by a narrow footpath to the left of the Mehrauli bus terminal. See also p. 66.

[3] The shrine of Khwaja Qutbuddin Bakhtiyar Kaki, which is visited by many devotees. His title 'Kaki' is said to derive from the small cakes ('Kaki') he was fed on during the 40 days' *chihal* or fast. This Chisti saint migrated to Delhi from Iran. His date of birth is not known, but he died in 1235.

to the throne, but he did his best to revive the empire during his short reign. He made peace with the Marathas and the Rajputs and restored order in the Punjab. He travelled from north to south and south to north incessantly and never actually stayed in Delhi at all. He was a very generous man and gave away many lands. For this reason he was called *Be-khabar* or the Heedless King.[1] Near him also lies Shah Alam who reigned from 1759 to 1806. He began his reign as a fugitive in Bihar, and ended it as a pensioner of the British Government. He came back to Delhi in 1772 and for a time was successful with the help of his minister Mirza Najaf Khan. But after Najaf Khan's death his nobles quarrelled and he was blinded by the Rohilla chief Ghulam Qadir Khan. Madhav Rao Sindhia[2] rescued him but after that he only enjoyed a nominal authority. Shah Alam was a poet and wrote a touching poem about his blindness. Between his grave and Bahadur Shah I's grave is a space reserved for Bahadur Shah II. Next to Shah Alam lies Akbar Shah II, who reigned from 1806 to 1837.

Close to the Dargah is the palace of Bahadur Shah II, the last Emperor. You can still see the gateway, but the rest of the palace is in ruins. [3] Bahadur Shah came here in the rains every year. He used to hunt in the country round, and he always went out in procession at the festival of Punkahs in August.[4] Bahadur Shah is buried in Rangoon.[5]

If you walk through the bazaar you will come to a fine tank with

---

[1] *Be-khabar* means literally 'without information'.

[2] For Najaf Khan, see also note 3 on p. 3 and p. 10. Mahadji (Madhav Rao) Sindhia belonged to the family of one of the five prominent Maratha chieftains (he joined the Maratha king's service in 1716) and had his capital at Gwalior. The Mughal rulers gave him the title of Regent after 1772. He died in 1794. The British army won Delhi after defeating the Maratha army under his great-nephew in 1803 at the battle of Patparganj.

[3] This is called Zafar Mahal — Bahadur Shah II's pen-name was 'Zafar' (Victory).

[4] The festival of Punkahs (fans), or Pankha Mela, also called the Phulwalon ki Sair (Procession of Flower Sellers), was instituted in the 1720s as a tribute to the Mughal ruler from the flower sellers (both Hindu and Muslim) of Mehrauli. The decorated fans, which are carried in procession, are blessed at the Hindu temple of Jogmaya and the Muslim shrine of Qutbuddin Bakhtiyar Kaki. It was revived after Independence, and is usually held in the first week of October at Mehrauli.

[5] After the revolt of 1857, Bahadur Shah II (although a frail 82) was exiled by the British to Rangoon, just as they had despatched Napoleon to St. Helena.

red pavilions round it.[1] This was built by Iltutmish in the thirteenth century (1229–30). There are many more interesting monuments in Mehrauli, but these we must visit another time.

ADDITIONAL NOTES

Metcalfe's house. Near the tomb which Metcalfe used as a house there is a tower on a stony ridge. This is locally known as Metcalfe's Battery. But it is not a battery. It is a tower built by Metcalfe in order that he might have something to look at as he sat on the verandah of his house in the evening. The tomb was that of Mohammed Quli Khan, brother of Adham Khan, whose descendants sold it to Metcalfe. He did not disturb the grave or use the burial chamber.

Adham Khan's tomb. This was also used as a house by Mr Blake. He was the assistant to the Resident at Jaipur and was murdered there in 1827.

The Jumping Well. This has no historical associations, but it is interesting to visit.

In Mughal times, after the new city of Shahjahanabad had been built, Mehrauli became a country town. Many nobles had country houses here because the hilly country round was very good for sport. Many Delhi families still have houses here which they visit in the rains.[2]

15. SIRI

We will choose a day in the cold weather for this expedition for we shall have a lot of walking to do. We can drive out along the Qutb road[3] as far as the turning to the Hauz Khas. A little way beyond this

---

[1] The tank is called Hauz Shamsi (Shamsuddin's Tank).

[2] The tradition lives on. Many wealthy Delhi families have 'farmhouses' (actually houses with large gardens whose agricultural activity rarely extends beyond growing vegetables for their own use) in the Mehrauli area and entertain there in the winter on a lavish scale.

[3] To see the remains of the Siri walls, turn into the Asiad Village from Khelgaon (Games Village) Marg and take the circular drive round the village and out again; some remains can also be seen further east on the north side of Panchsheel Park, but the fields that Spear speaks of are now covered over by an electricity sub-station and the extensions of Panchsheel Park colony.

a new road turns off to the left and there is a signpost marked TO SIRI. Walk about half a mile along this road and you will come to the walls of Siri.[1] You can see the walls quite clearly from the Qutb road before you start to walk.

The walls in some places are quite complete and you can walk right round them. There are a number of towers and gates. They are about a mile and a half round. Inside there is today nothing but fields and crops. But once there was the great palace of Alauddin Khilji. Soon after Alauddin came to the throne in 1296 the Mongols invaded India and marched right to Delhi. They were then very fierce and uncivilized. Alauddin was not strong enough to fight them in the open, so he retired to the Qutb. The Mongols occupied and plundered all the suburbs of Delhi, and all the gardens and palaces of the nobles. At last the Mongols retreated because they were not strong enough to storm the walls of Delhi and they did not like the hot weather.[2] Alauddin determined that they should never plunder the suburbs and gardens again. So he built the fort of Siri to protect them. No one could plunder the suburbs unless they first took the fort of Siri. Inside the fort Alauddin built a palace. In it was a hall which was famous throughout India and was called the Hall of a Thousand Pillars. We know that this Hall was in Siri, but we do not yet know its exact site. One day, perhaps, the archaeologists will find it for us with their spades.[3]

[1] A popular explanation for the name is that at the time of its construction, the Mongols launched another raid on Delhi. They were defeated and eight thousand Mongol heads were built into the walls of the fort – hence its rather macabre name 'Siri' from the Hindi for 'head' (Vohra, *Delhi!*, p. 176). Similar legends are attached to various towers, such as the Chor Minar in present-day Hauz Khas Enclave; Bamber Gascoigne reproduces a 1632 drawing of a tower of heads by Peter Mundy (*The Great Moghuls*, p. 76).

[2] Having first described the thirteenth-century Mongols as fierce and uncivilized, Spear here makes them sound like wilting memsahibs! See p. 70 for more on 'the Mongol menace'.

[3] Hazaar Sutoon (1000 Pillars) Halls figure at Siri (see p. 70) and at Muhammed Tughlaq's Bijay Mandal (see p. 72), just as the Chahal/Chalis Sutoon (40 pillars) Hall figures later in Safavid Isfahan and Mughal Agra and Delhi. The Sanskrit treatise on architecture, *Vastu Sastra* (written around the time of the birth of Christ) contains a chapter on *Mandapas* (Halls) which discusses the number of pillars to be used (usually 500 or 1000). The Palace at Siri was forever buried under the Asiad Village before the archaeologists could get at it with their spades. During construction of the Village (1982), many remains from earlier centuries were discovered but built over.

Alauddin was a great warrior and did not have time to live very much in Delhi. He it was who defeated the Rajputs and took Ranthambor and Chitor in 1303. But he is most famous for his campaign in the south. He conquered the Deccan and added it to the Delhi empire. To celebrate this victory, he began a Minar which was to be twice as high as the Qutb Minar, but he did not live to finish it. He also wanted to build a great mosque. But Siri was not large enough for a great mosque as well as a palace. For this reason Alauddin decided to enlarge the mosque at the Qutb as we have already seen.[1] His monument there is the Alai Darwaza. In his time Delhi became the Capital, not only of Hindustan, but of all India.[2]

Beyond Siri you will see the walls of a large enclosure.

This is Chiragh Delhi, where there is a saint's shrine. The walls were built in the eighteenth century by a nobleman and the villagers took shelter there for safety. There is a tomb in Chiragh Delhi which is probably that of Bahlol Lodi (died 1489).[3]

Now we must retrace our steps back to the Qutb road. As we come near the road there are two buildings of interest. The first is a small tower which is known as the Chor Minar. Its present name is due to the fact that it is said that thieves used to be hanged from it. It was probably built in the reign of Alauddin. Near here there lived a colony of Mongols who had settled down in Delhi.[4] When the Mongol army came to Delhi they were tempted to join their brothers. Alauddin thought they were a danger to the city. He was a fierce and

---

[1] It is difficult to believe that Siri was 'not large enough'; Alauddin obviously chose to 'focus on the monument that remained symbolically paramount' (Asher, p. 5).

[2] 'Hindustan' means north India. Alauddin conquered the Deccan but not the far south, which remained under the Pandya rulers of Madurai.

[3] Chiragh Delhi (Lamp of Delhi) is named after Nasiruddin Mohammed, called Chiragh-e-Dehli (d. 1356), a disciple of Sheikh Nizamuddin Auliya. The settlement around his shrine used to be surrounded by a high wall until the 1950s. Today some *chhattris* and a beautiful southern gateway survive; shops and houses have been built against the wall, and the village is entered by the ruined northern gateway. The layout of the village is that of a miniature medieval town. The tomb of Bahlol Lodi is near that of the saint.

[4] Chor Minar is in Hauz Khas (east), reached by taking a right turning off the road from Hauz Khas Market to Lakshman Public School off the Panchsheel Road. The area in west Delhi called 'Mongolpuri' is supposed to be the thirteenth-century Mongol colony.

ruthless king and so he killed them all. It was said that their heads were stuck on spikes fixed to this tower as a warning to traitors.

The other building is quite near to the Chor Minar. From a distance it looks just like a long wall. But when you come up to it, you will find that it is an Idgah mosque.[1] There is an inscription on the wall, dated 1404 A.D. This was six years after Timur had come to India and taken Delhi. It records the building of the mosque and mentions the desolation of the city caused by him. Compare this Idgah mosque with the present Idgah near Delhi city,[2] and you will realize that the people who built it were very poor. This was the best that they could build after Timur had plundered Delhi.

All around you will see stones and walls which tell of the greatness of the city which stood here. They are the remains of the houses and palaces of the city. When you get back to the Qutb road you are on the outskirts of the city. The country all around and specially on the other side of the road was covered with gardens and palaces and tanks.

Just here, close to the main road, are some old buildings. Close by is a little mosque which is called the *Nili Masjid* or Blue Mosque.[3] It was built in the time of the Lodis and it still has some beautiful blue tiles on its dome. These tiles came from Persia at the end of the 15th century and were put on the domes of buildings. When the Mughals came and had plenty of money, they used marble instead.

ADDITIONAL NOTES

An excursion to Siri shows the reality of the Mongol menace to India in several ways. First it shows how the fortress of Siri was built to repel the Mongols and how it was necessary to protect the suburbs of Delhi. Then the Chor Minar and its story shows the terror which the Mongol invaders

---

[1] Also in Hauz Khas (east).

[2] 'The present Idgah' is a much larger structure, built for Shahjahan's city. Idgahs are located west of and at a distance from the city. This is a little difficult to appreciate now because this building (along the right hand side of the Rani of Jhansi Marg from Connaught Place to Sadar Bazaar) has, over the last 100 years, been hemmed in by urban sprawl.

[3] This is just off Aurobindo Marg at the T-junction where the left turning leads to Khelgaon Marg.

inspired. If you read Persian poetry you can realize this still better from the poems of Amir Khusrau, who once was taken prisoner by them.[1] Thirdly, the Wall Mosque shows to what poverty Delhi was reduced when the Mongols under Timur at last took Delhi in 1398. The great work of the Slave, Khilji and Tughlaq dynasties was to save India from the Mongol terror which at that time devastated Persia. Though many of these kings were hard and ruthless men, in that respect they did a great service to India. Remember that the Mongols of Chinghiz Khan were wild horsemen from Central Asia who despised cities and destroyed all that they came across. It was in the fifteenth century that they adopted the culture of Persia. Babur was a descendant of Timur, but he was a cultured, honourable and tolerant man. His arrival in India was on the whole a blessing. The conquest of India by Chinghiz Khan and his immediate successors would have been an unmixed evil.

Siri. Alauddin got the idea of a Hall of a Thousand Pillars from the south. When he captured Madura, he found such a hall there, and, as he always wanted to have the best of everything, he determined to build a hall like it in Delhi.[2] Later as you will see, Mohammed Tughlaq built another for his palace.

16. THE BIJAY MANDAL

The Bijay Mandal is about a mile from the Qutb near the Delhi road. In order to get to it you should drive along the Qutb road until you

[1] 'At the time that the author was a captive in the hands of the Mongols [1285], may such days never return! Travelling in a sandy desert, where the heat made my head boil like a cauldron, I and the man who was with me on horseback arrived thirsty at a stream by the roadside . . . I just moistened my lips and obtained a little relief from my exhaustion. But my thirsty guard dismounted, both he and his horse drank their fill of water and expired immediately' (*Dewal Rani Khizr Khan*). Elsewhere Khusrau describes a Mongol attack: 'The Mongol hordes marched out from Turkestan [with] fifty thousand skilled and fearful horsemen, so that the mountain trembled due to the wind of that army and the dwellers of the foot of the mountain . . . were blown off . . . and fell into the valley of the Ganga. The lightning of the Mongol's prowess reached these too and raised up smoke from the towns of Hindustan' (*Khazain-ul-Futuh*, p. 20).

[2] There is an old tradition of building 1000-pillared halls, but the Airakkal ('Thousand pillars' in Tamil) Mandapa (Hall) at Madurai's Minakshi Temple was built in the seventeenth century – four hundred years later – so Alauddin could not have got the *idea* from Madurai.

have passed the turning to the Hauz Khas. A little way beyond this
you will see on the left-hand side of the road a large square-looking
tower with a building joined to it. This is the Bijay Mandal and you
will soon come to a little kachcha road with a notice TO THE BIJAY
MANDAL.[1]

What is the Bijay Mandal? It is all that is left of the Palace of
Mohammed Tughlaq. You will remember that Mohammed Tughlaq
succeeded his father Ghiyasuddin in 1325. He did not like his father's
city of Tughlaqabad, so he decided to return to the old city of Delhi.
But that city had grown too big for the walls of Lal Kot. Alauddin
had built the fort of Siri and in between Siri and Mehrauli were
houses and gardens and shops. But they were unfortified and un-
protected from the Mongol raids. Mohammed Shah decided that he
would make this place his capital. So he built a great wall from Siri
to Lal Kot and made three cities into one. He called this city
Jahanpanah ('the refuge of the world') and in the middle he built his
palace and mosque.

You can still see one of the city walls if you walk to the village
of Khirki. You can do this either from the Bijay Mandal or the Qutb.
The path is across fields, and the villagers will direct you.[2] In the wall
you will notice sluices or gates for water.[3] The reason for these
water-gates is that Mohammed Shah made a great lake or tank
between his city of Jahanpanah and Tughlaqabad. These gates let the
water in and out. The lake must have been very beautiful. Today
you can see that the land is very flat and easy to flood. Now it is very
fertile.

[1] The Bijay Mandal (Victory Area) is in a large enclosure south of Sarvapriya Vihar
opposite the Panchsheel Club.

[2] To reach Khirki drive south along Aurobindo Marg, crossing the Outer Ring
Road by the IIT. Turn left at the signpost to Saket, and Khirki is after the Press
Enclave on the left. Sections of the wall of Siri can be seen along this road.

[3] The sluices are a few yards further east from Khirki Village, along the same road.
It is a ruined structure which still conveys a sense of rugged grandeur. Called Satpula,
meaning seven bridges or seven-sectioned bridge, you will notice that it only has *six*
arches; this is because the builders of the time were counting the supporting pillars,
not the arches as we would tend to do.

As at Hauz Khas, there was a *madarsa* here. There is a long tradition in India of
associating seats of learning with inspirational physical surroundings, whether man-
made such as this water-based architecture, or natural such as the later rural idyll of
Tagore's Shantiniketan.

Now we will look at the Bijay Mandal itself.[1] Close to the building on the Qutb road side are some foundations which have been excavated. These are the remains of the royal baths or hammam and the zenana. Next we will mount the tower.[2] From it you get a fine view of the countryside. It is said that Mohammed Shah used to sit on this roof and review the troops who marched about below. In those days the tower had a pavilion on the top of it.

You will find that the building which joins the tower has a large platform or *chabutra*. You can see the places where the pillars stood. This was the Diwan-i-Khas or Hall of Private Audience, where Mohammed Shah consulted his counsellors. Many matters of state were discussed here. On one side of the platform you can see the remains of a sloping path which ran up from the ground to the platform. It is steep, but has no steps. That was to enable the royal elephants to bring the king up to his private apartments. Behind the platform are the remains of rooms which were the private apartments of the king. In these rooms are two stone vaults or holes in the ground. These were treasure chambers. When the archaeologists opened them a few years ago they found at the bottom some gold coins of south India. Probably Alauddin brought them back with him from his campaigns in the south.

If you go through these rooms to the other side you will see that there is a level space on the ground with holes in regular lines. This is all that remains of the Diwan-i-Am or Hall of Public Audience. Until it was excavated a few years ago we knew nothing about it. This hall was called the Hall of a Thousand Pillars.[3] Alauddin built a Hall of a Thousand Pillars in his palace at Siri a few years before. Mohammed Tughlaq was determined that his palace should be as fine as Alauddin's so he built a Hall of a Thousand Pillars also. It is a very large hall. We cannot see all of it today because part of it is now covered by a cemetery.[4]

Close to the Bijay Mandal is a village and close to the village is a

---

[1] See first paragraph of Additional Notes (p. 73) for more on the Bijay Mandal.

[2] This is a tower which you *are* still allowed to climb: hurry before someone changes the rules . . .

[3] See second paragraph of Additional Notes (p. 74) and p. 70 (Siri) for more on the Hall of a Thousand Pillars.

[4] Prayers and sessions of religious music are held here on Thursday nights.

large mosque.[1] This was the Jama Masjid of Jahanpanah and here Mohammed Shah went in state to pray. In those days the walls were covered with plaster and decorated with texts and paint. Today all these things have gone, but we can still admire the great courtyard and the fine proportions of the mosque. Until a few years ago the mosque was occupied by the village which is called Begumpur. The Archaeological Department moved the villagers out and gave them new houses just outside.

Mohammed Shah was a very clever and brave king, but he was also cruel and changeable. It was he who moved the capital to Daulatabad in the Deccan and took all the inhabitants of Delhi with him.[2] A few years later he grew tired of Daulatabad and moved all the people back to Delhi. Ibn Batuta, the great Arab traveller, was the Kazi of Delhi for some years under Mohammed Shah. He thus describes the king:

> This king is of all men the fondest of making gifts and shedding blood. His gate is never without some poor man enriched or some living man executed, and stories are current amongst the people of his generosity and courage and of his cruelty and violence towards criminals.[3]

ADDITIONAL NOTES

The Bijay Mandal. The tomb standing close to one corner of the Bijay Mandal has nothing to do with Mohammed Shah's palace. It was built later.

The Hall of a Thousand Pillars had two storeys, and the pillars were of wood. That is why they have disappeared, and you can now see only the sockets into which they were fixed. If you count the lines of sockets and allow for the portion covered by the cemetery you will find that there

---

[1] See p. 74 for more on the Begumpuri Masjid, built by Khan-e-Jahan Telingani.

[2] Daulatabad/Deogiri is a magnificent fort close to the Ellora caves, which changed hands frequently between the twelfth and eighteenth centuries.

[3] Ibn Batuta (1304–78), born in Morocco, was an indefatigable traveller. He spent eight years at the court of Mohammed Tughlaq, who sent him to China as an ambassador in 1342. His *Rehla* (Travels) gives a vivid account of life at the time; he well summed up Mohammed Tughlaq as 'a brilliant but capricious ruler who has never ceased to be the object of controversy among historians'.

were very nearly 500 pillars on each floor. For the origin of Halls of a Thousand Pillars see under Siri.

There are some excavations between the Mandal and the mosque. These are thought to have been part of the royal stables.

The mosque. Many large mosques near Delhi and elsewhere were occupied by villagers in the eighteenth century. The reason was the insecurity of those times. If there was any stone enclosure large enough the villagers moved into it for protection. If there was none they built mud walls round their villages. They could then defy looters, and would bargain with revenue officers about their land tax from behind their walls. Soldiers spent much of their time going round the country collecting revenue, because the villagers would not pay unless force was used, and they saw that it was useless to resist.

17. HAUZ KHAS

Today we shall go to another well-known place near Delhi. You can go either by bus or tonga, for there is a good road all the way. Between two and three miles from Safdarjang's tomb on the Qutb road there is a group of tombs, and here the road to Hauz Khas[1] turns off to the right. It is plainly marked with a signpost. The Hauz Khas is at the end of this road, about a mile from the main road. [2] You enter the enclosure by a gateway and immediately find yourself in a garden, well cared for by the Archaeological Department.

First we will look at the Hauz Khas itself. It is a great space nearly square. Two sides are nearly half a mile long and the other two nearly three furlongs.[3] You can trace all the banks of the tank quite easily.

[1] Hauz Khas lies to the west of Aurobindo Marg between the Ring Road and the Outer Ring Road (Abdul Gamel Nasser Marg at this point). If you would like to approach on foot, it is a 15-minute walk in the Deer Park through the Rose Garden from the Outer Ring Road (here Olof Palme Marg).

[2] The monuments of Hauz Khas are to be found at the end of Hauz Khas Village, a maze of lanes lined with clothes and furniture boutiques, craft shops and restaurants developed in the 1980s.

[3] The royal ('Khas') tank ('Hauz') can be seen from Firoz Shah's tomb and the *madarsa*; stone steps lead down to the tank. A furlong is an eighth of a mile, so it measures almost half a mile by three-eighths of a mile, according to Spear's measurements. Delhi Tourism is currently (1993) attempting to develop the site as a tourist attraction, filling the tank and staging Indian dance evenings against the illuminated backdrop of the monuments.

In the centre is an island with the ruins of a pavilion on it. If you go there after the winter rains or in the monsoon you will see water in the corner nearest to you: otherwise the tank will probably be dry. This tank was filled by rain-water which drained off the ridge about a mile away.[1] Behind that ridge there is now the new cantonment.[2] If you walk round the tank (which I hope you will do) you will find a gap in the bank on the side opposite to the main buildings (and nearest to the ridge). This is probably where the water came in. In the old days the tank was filled during the rains and it must then have been a very fine sheet of water. We have nothing like it in Delhi today. In the hot weather Ferishta[3] says that it dried up round the banks and then it was sown with sugarcane, cucumbers, green melons and pumpkins. When Timur had defeated Mohammed Tughlaq and Mallu Khan he encamped on the banks of the Hauz Khas before entering the city of Delhi. He says that it was so large 'that a man cannot shoot an arrow across it.' Probably the Hauz Khas was neglected in the troubles after Timur's invasion. It has never been used since. The tank is very fertile, and if you visit it during the cold weather you will see the floor of the tank waving with crops of various kinds.

The Hauz Khas was built by Alauddin and was the private or royal tank of the king. That is why it is called the Hauz Khas. Firoz Shah Tughlaq repaired it. He must have loved it very much, for he built a madarsa on its banks and his own tomb in one corner. The madarsa forms the two ranges of buildings at the corner of the tank. You will notice that on top of the chief buildings are halls of pillars. Underneath there are rows of rooms with a verandah in front. In some places the verandah has fallen down, but in others it is still

[1] The skills of the thirteenth-century engineers at Hauz Khas harnessed Delhi's assets: the southwest–northeast Ridge, the regular monsoons, the local sandstone and the regulated canal network, e.g. at Wazirabad and Satpula, to give the successive towns at Delhi a fertile and green hinterland. Today the fields have been taken over by housing estates, and the Ridge which Spear refers to has also largely been levelled. The Ridge 'about a mile away' refers to the area of Dhaula Kuan.

[2] The present cantonment. This was laid out at the same time as Lutyens' New Delhi.

[3] Mohammed Qasim 'Ferishta' (c.1560 – c.1620) was born near the Caspian Sea, and came to India as a child. In the service of the Sultan of Bijapur, he wrote a book on indigenous Indian medicine, and an excellent history of India from the eleventh– seventeenth century, called 'Tarikh' (History) '-e-Ferishta'.

standing. The pillared halls were lecture rooms, where the students sat with the *maulvis*, and the rooms below were the cells of the students. You can count up these rooms for yourself and see how many students the madarsa could hold. Very likely there were two students to each room. At one end of the building was a mosque which no doubt the students used. This madarsa was a college for the study of Arabic. It was founded by Firoz Shah and was the largest and best college of its time. This college also was ruined by Timur's invasion. In those days Delhi was a far greater seat of learning than it is today.[1]

At the corner of the college stands the tomb of Firoz Shah himself. It is a square, strong-looking building, but most of its decoration has disappeared. Inside is the grave of the king, and beside him lie two of his family. He was nearly ninety years old when he died in 1388. In the garden outside the college are a number of little domes supported by pillars, or *chhattris*. We do not know exactly what they were, but some of them are probably tombs. There is also quite a large pillared hall. It was perhaps a *majlis khana* or assembly hall for the college.

As you walk round the tank you will see a number of large tombs. These were tombs of noblemen of the Tughlaq period. Most of them have no inscription and so we do not know exactly who were buried in them. Near the Qutb road there is another group of tombs. They were built later, in the fifteenth century, and they are also nameless.[2]

ADDITIONAL NOTES

When you visit the Hauz Khas, you should explore for yourself the different parts of the madarsa – the lecture rooms, assembly halls, students' rooms and mosque. This will make it easier for you to imagine what a great madarsa was like. During the Sultanate Delhi was a great seat of learning.

---

[1] An ironic statement for Spear to make as a lecturer at the prestigious St Stephen's College, and it is debatable whether his fellow academics, either there or at the fledgling Delhi University (such as the innovative Vice-Chancellor, Maurice Gwyer), would have agreed with him!

[2] Spear is probably referring to the two tombs which you pass on your way to Hauz Khas from Aurobindo Marg. These *are* 'nameless', but they have long been known as Dadi-Poti (Grandmother – Grand-daughter).

Iltutmish was the first great patron of learning and most of the later kings also encouraged scholars. Scholars were rewarded by pensions and royal gifts. Colleges were supported by the grant of rent-free lands.[1] After Timur's invasion many scholars fled or were killed; the lands were seized by others and so the college revenue ceased, and then the colleges were deserted. Delhi became a seat of learning again under Shahjahan and Aurangzeb, but in the troubles of the eighteenth century the colleges lost their endowments again. While visiting the Hauz Khas you can picture to yourself what college education was like in mediaeval India. The madarsas, like the one at Hauz Khas, were the universities of the time. Here Arabic was studied, and then the Koran, and Muslim theology and philosophy and law. From these colleges came the *maulvis* and *kazis* of the empire. Persian was studied by the nobles. But they usually had private tutors and did not go to colleges. The commercial classes (merchants, shopkeepers, etc.) learnt reading and writing in their vernacular (Hindi or Urdu) and had their own schools. There were no great Sanskrit colleges in Delhi and the Hindus who wanted to study Sanskrit seriously went to Benares.

The buildings at Hauz Khas are typical examples of the Tughlaq style. Note the strong square pillars, the few arches, the absence of ornament. Note also the sloping walls of Firoz Shah's tomb.[2]

A word of caution! There is a big drop from the madarsa to the tank below. Be careful that in your excitement you do not fall over!

18. TUGHLAQABAD

You can see Tughlaqabad in the distance as you go along in the train towards Agra, or in a bus along the Mathura road, or from the Qutb Minar. But it is not so easy to get to it.[3] Yet it is one of the best places to visit near Delhi in the cold weather. There are three ways of reaching it. Firstly, you can go by train to Tughlaqabad station (Badarpur village) and walk about two miles to Tughlaqabad. Secondly, you can go by road along the Mathura road to Badarpur, and then turn sharp right to Tughlaqabad. Thirdly, you can go to the Qutb and there turn left to Tughlaqabad. The most interesting thing is to

---

[1] These rent-free lands were known as *madad-i-maash*. See p. 26, note 2, about Firoz Shah's support for men of learning who had been forced to flee their homelands.

[2] See p. 104 for an analysis of Tughlaq architectural style.

[3] It is now easy to reach Tughlaqabad (on the Mehrauli-Badarpur Road) and it is convenient to combine it with a trip to the Qutb Minar area.

make a round trip by road – that is to go one way and return the other. That is what we will do.

We will start along the Mathura road. After you have passed Nizamuddin you should keep a look-out on the left-hand side of the road. You will see a lot of brick-fields and if you are sharp you will also see some towers about twenty feet high shaped like this: They stand in fields at intervals of about two miles and are *Kos-minars* or mile-stones.[1] They were placed by Akbar along the Grand Trunk road all the way from Agra to Ambala.

Fig. 6

At Badarpur we turn right, cross the B.B. & C.I. railway,[2] and soon come to Tughlaqabad. We will drive right on until we come to a tomb with a marble dome and a wall round it on the left-hand side of the road. Now look around you. Close by you are the walls of the citadel or Fort of Tughlaqabad. There is a gateway, and if you go inside you will see the ground strewn with ruins of every sort. You can climb up into the fort and sit on the battlements and look at the view. Here the founder, Ghiyasuddin Tughlaq, often sat and looked over the plains of Delhi. See how high and strong the walls are. See how grim and stern they look! See too, that the walls do not stand straight up, but are sloping. This was to make them stronger still.

Now we will look at the marble tomb. We walk along a little causeway of stone and enter a fortified enclosure. Inside this stands a tomb of red stone with a white marble dome. You can see this dome from the Qutb Minar.[3] This tomb is that of Ghiyasuddin Tughlaq, the founder of the Tughlaq dynasty. Beside him lies his wife Makh Dumai Jahan, and his son Mohammed Tughlaq,[4] who built the Bijay

---

[1] A minar is a tower, and a kos was a measure of distance (approximately two miles).

[2] The B.B. & C.I. Railway came up to Mathura, where one changed to the G.I.P. line for Delhi. After 1857 the East India Railway Company and the Great Indian Peninsula Railway Company began the awesome task of building railway lines across the length and breadth of India. They were joined in 1891 by the B.B. & C.I. (Bombay, Baroda and Central India) Railway. As in Britain, the various railways in India were all privately owned until Independence, after which they were nationalized. As in Britain also, great romance is attached to this golden age of rail travel.

[3] No longer.

[4] The tombs are not marked but it is easy to work out which must be which: Ghiyasuddin lies in the centre, his wife on one side and his son on the other.

Mandal and the Begumpur mosque, and died at Thatta in Sind in 1351.

Now why is the tomb fortified and why is there a causeway to it? Look round carefully and you will see that the land is very flat and the road[1] is raised some feet above it. On one side is the city and on another are stony hills. In this space between the city and the hills was a lake or tank, and Ghiyasuddin's tomb was in the middle of this lake. The causeway was necessary to reach this tomb. The wall round the tomb was built to protect it from Mongol raiders who might loot it. Look again, and you will see that a stream runs into the plain from the city.[2] This supplied the lake with water. Besides this there was the monsoon rain which came down from the hills. At the end of this level plain towards Badarpur there is a bund which kept the water in on that side. On the hill opposite is a small fort, called Adilabad. It was meant to protect the lake on that side.

If you are feeling very energetic you can walk right round the city of Tughlaqabad. It is about three-and-a-half miles round.

Ghiyasuddin Tughlaq was one of the *Maliks* of Alauddin Khilji. He was Governor of Samana under Alauddin's son.[3] When Khusrau Khan, 'the sweeper king',[4] seized the throne, he marched to Delhi, and defeated and killed him in 1321.[5] In those days the Mongols were very fierce and destructive, and every one feared them very much. Ghiyasuddin decided to build a fortress which would be too strong for them to take. So he built Tughlaqabad in these stony hills and finished it in less than four years. Because there was little water there he made the lake which I have just described.

---

[1] i.e. the Mehrauli-Badarpur Road.

[2] No longer. The landscape around Tughlaqabad has changed greatly since Spear's time, chiefly because of extensive stone-quarrying. However, thanks to the (indirectly!) beneficent influence of the many nearby defence installations, the area immediately around Ghiyasuddin's tomb is kept blessedly free of encroaching buildings (unlike many other monuments such as Sultan Ghari's tomb or Hauz Khas).

[3] Mubarak Khan, son of Alauddin Khilji, reigned during 1316-20. Samana is north of Panipat.

[4] Khusrau Khan was a man of obscure birth who won the trust of Mubarak Khan and then usurped his throne and murdered him.

[5] Ghiyasuddin, Governor of nearby Samana, marched to Delhi in outrage, overthrew Khusrau Khan and then killed him, mindful perhaps of the contemporary saying 'Ya takht, ya takhta' ('Either the throne or the coffin').

Ghiyasuddin was a great soldier and a stern ruler. He restored order in Hindustan and repulsed the Mongols. Then he marched to Bengal and put down a rebellion there. At this time he quarrelled with Nizamuddin, as related in Chapter 8. On his return his son Mohammed went out to meet him at Afghanpur. Ghiyas sat under a pavilion and reviewed his troops. After some time Mohammed retired and elephants were brought before the king. One of them knocked against a wooden pillar and the whole pavilion fell on the king and killed him. Mohammed said it was an accident, but many people thought he had arranged it all on purpose.

Nizamuddin prophesied that Tughlaqabad would be the abode of jackals and Gujars,[1] and so it turned out. Mohammed Shah did not like Tughlaqabad and built Jahanpanah. The city was deserted and today there is only a little village there – of Gujars.[2]

ADDITIONAL NOTES

When you go on this expedition, read in your books about Ghiyasuddin Tughlaq. He was a fine and strong character, for he did not seek the throne and only marched to Delhi when his master's son had been murdered and the empire was in confusion. He restored order and saved India for a time from the Mughal invasions.

There was one great defect about Tughlaqabad, that was lack of water. Ghiyas made the lake in order to remedy this defect. But the wells of Tughlaqabad only had bitter (or brackish) water, and there must have been much sickness. This lack of good water was probably one of the chief reasons why Mohammed Tughlaq abandoned Tughlaqabad.

In the city wall near to the bund which enclosed the lake on the Badarpur side there is a gateway. All the upper stone-work has fallen away and just the arch is left. You can see the keystone of this arch very clearly. It is an excellent example of the true arch with a keystone. It also illustrates the strength of the true arch, because though all the building above it has fallen this arch still stands.[3]

[1] See Afterword for more on the suspense-filled story of Nizamuddin's prophecy and how Mohammed Tughlaq came to the throne.

[2] Gujars are nomads and herdsmen.

[3] As one travels east on the Mehrauli-Badarpur Road, the arch can be seen on the left, opposite a new Shiva temple, at the point where the road dips beyond Tughlaqabad.

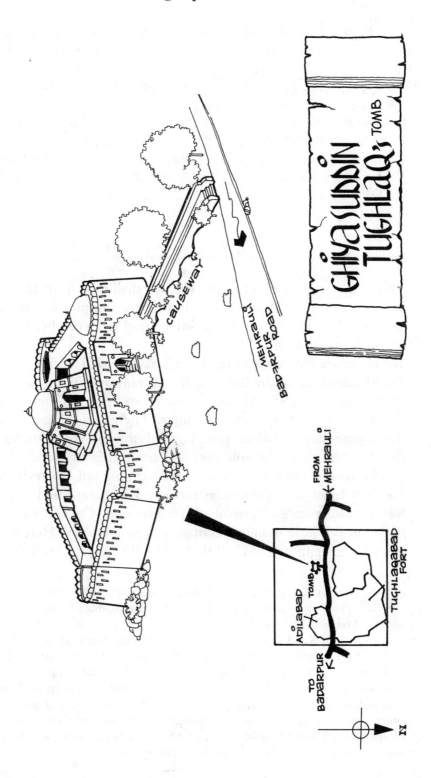

GHIYASUDDIN TUGHLAQ; TOMB

CAUSEWAY

MEHRAULI BADARPUR ROAD

FROM ←MEHRAULI

ADILABAD

TOMB

TUGHLAQABAD FORT

TO BADARPUR

N

The buildings of Tughlaqabad are remarkable for their strength and solidity and for their sloping walls. Their effect has been compared to that of ancient Egyptian architecture, which is equally strong and solid, and also has sloping walls. They reflect the whole spirit of the Tughlaq dynasty and the character of its founder, Ghiyasuddin Tughlaq.[1]

The walls of Badarpur were built in the early eighteenth century as a serai.[2] The villagers moved into the enclosure, as in so many other places, when the time of troubles began. Badarpur marked the first full stage from Delhi to Agra along the Grand Trunk road. Badarpur is eleven miles from the Delhi gate.

19. SURAJ KUND[3]

This is the longest excursion which we shall take from Delhi. You have to walk some distance and most of the country is bare of trees and rocky. So it is best to go to Suraj Kund in December or January when the weather is cold.

There are two ways of reaching Suraj Kund. The first is to go to Tughlaqabad station by the B.B. & C.I. railway. Or else you can go to Badarpur along the Mathura road. From there you must walk for about two miles across open country. There is a village about half way where they will direct you. Towards the end you come to rocky country, and then suddenly you will come to a small valley with a bund across it. On the other side is a charming jhil. Over the hill on the right-hand side of the valley is the tank of Suraj Kund. The other way is this. You go by road to Tughlaqabad. On the side nearest Badarpur is a little temple and dharmsala in a hollow. Here you will see a large signpost — TO SURAJ KUND. A path leads for about

---

[1] See Chapter 22 for an analysis of the Tughlaq architectural style.

[2] Badarpur Serai is worth a visit. It is west of the Mathura Road, at its junction with the Mehrauli-Badarpur Road.

[3] Suraj (Sun) Kund (Lake) is a tank dedicated to the Sun God. It is now easy to reach (off the Faridabad road) but technically in the neighbouring state of Haryana, no longer part of Delhi. The whole area has changed beyond recognition: relentless quarrying of stone for Delhi's mushrooming building industry has flattened out many hills, and the area around Suraj Kund has been developed as a recreational centre, rather overwhelming the original historical site. Every February it is the venue for the enormous Suraj Kund Crafts Mela (fair). Thus what Spear thinks of as a pleasantly solitary outing now risks becoming a Delhi Disneyland!

two miles straight to the great tank. This is now well marked out so
that you need no guide. There are always some country people at
the temple if you want help of any sort.

What are we going to see? Suraj Kund is the site of the oldest
city of Delhi of which there are any visible remains. This city was
built by Anang Pal, a Tomar Rajput, in the early years of the eleventh
century (about 1020 A.D.).[1] It was probably occupied for about a
century when the city was moved to the Qutb. We have no records
of this time, and so we can only guess at the reasons for the choice
of this site. You will see that all the country round is very rocky and
barren, and very hot in the summer. There is little water. But it is
also very defensible. Now think what was happening in India about
1020. It was the time of Mahmud of Ghazni's[2] invasions. He spread
terror over all northern India. Very likely Anang Pal chose this site
because it was very strong and out-of-the-way, and so he hoped that
he would be safe from Mahmud of Ghazni.

Now we will start our walk – choosing the path from Badarpur.[3]
This brings us to a small rocky valley, with the bund and the jhil.
The stream which runs down this valley is very small. But the city
depended on it for water. So the bund was built to keep the water
in. First we climb the hill on the right-hand side of the bund. When
you reach the top you will see just below you the great tank of Suraj
Kund. It is a great semi-circle of masonry. There are steps all round
the semi-circle. In the middle of the straight side are the steps of a

[1] The Tomars were a Rajput dynasty who ruled in north India from the eighth
century A.D. Coins dated 1132, marked with Anang Pal's name, have been found but
there are two or three different genealogies of the period, each giving different dates
and sequences for the Tomar kings.

[2] The kingdom of Ghazni was founded in 962. Mahmud expanded it as far west
as Azerbaijan. On his eastern front he repeatedly plundered Indian cities and defeated
an alliance of Indian rulers (including the Tomar ruler of Delhi) in 1018. Later in the
century, the Tomars supported his Ghaznavid (i.e. from Ghazni) successors in the
Punjab. In 1151, another Afghan dynasty, the Ghurids (from Ghur) sacked Ghazni
and pushed the Ghaznavids out of Afghanistan, forcing them to retreat to their
stronghold in the Punjab. In the same year the Chauhans (now properly called the
Chahamanas but still popularly known as Chauhans) defeated the Tomars of Delhi.
The Chauhans held the plains between the Indus and the Ganga valleys until
Mohammed Ghuri defeated the Chauhan Prithviraj III at the 1192 Battle of Tarain
(?north of Meerut or near Bhatinda).

[3] From the Badkal Lake road, look for the 'Anangpur' sign on the right, opposite
the Greenfields Colony sign.

large building. This was a temple to Surya, which gives its name to the tank. You will see that at one corner there is a gap in the masonry. This is where water flowed into the tank. There is still a small spring there. Further round there is a gap in the steps and a stone road runs down to the water. This was

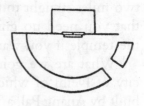

FIG. 7

for the elephants when they came down to the water to bathe. There is always water in the tank unless the season is very dry. Suraj Kund is the largest and finest Hindu monument in all Delhi.

From Suraj Kund we will go back to the bund and the jhil. Climb the hill on the other side. At once you will come across the remains of a city.[1] There are stones and walls and pillars. There is also one well. I never found another. What does this show? It shows that the city was very short of water. It explains why the king made tanks and lakes to keep the water in.

Next we go back to the bund and the jhil in the valley, but it is not yet time to return, for there is more to see. We must walk up the valley and follow the stream. The valley is very pretty, with palm trees and crops. It is about a mile long. After a time the valley enters a gorge, where the rocks on either side are quite high.[2] Here there is a Gujar village. Just beyond the village there is a wall across the valley. Anang Pal built this too. It is easy to climb up this bund and walk upon it. If you look carefully you will see that there is a gateway (or sluice) in the bund. This gate could be opened or shut, and so the flow of water was regulated. On the rocks above the bund is a chhattri.[3] I expect Anang Pal used to sit there and enjoy the cool breezes.

As you stand on the bund, look at the country around. The narrow valley opens out and forms a circular plain or basin in the hills. It is very fertile and green with crops. You can see the villagers working at their wells and in the fields. In the middle of the plain is a group

[1] There are still some traces of fortifications.

[2] The valley is still as Spear describes it except that quarrying has widened the gorge.

[3] The villagers of Anangpur continued to regulate the flow of water by operating the 1000-year old sluice gates until 1990. Recently, land has changed hands and some 'farmhouses' have been built. The *chhattri* collapsed some years ago and its massive pillars are still lying where they fell.

of trees. This is the village of Anangpur.[1] It is named after Anang Pal. It shows how the memory of great men continues in the countryside long after other people have forgotten about them. All this smiling plain was a great lake in the time of Anang Pal. The big bund was built to keep the water in. It was this lake which supplied the city with water during the hot weather.

These ruins show us two things. First, that the time was one of great danger and insecurity, and secondly, that Anang Pal was a great and energetic king.

ADDITIONAL NOTES

When you visit Suraj Kund think of Mahmud of Ghazni, as it illustrates the fear which he inspired. Mahmud took and sacked Meerut, but he did not come to Delhi. So he was very near to Delhi. Perhaps Suraj Kund was too strong for him. There are certain practical points to notice about a visit to Suraj Kund. It is the most difficult of all the excursions, but it is one of the most worth while. You should visit it if you possibly can. The trip requires a whole day.[2] If you go from the temple at Tughlaqabad be sure that you do not stray from the path on the way. The rocks are so confusing that you can easily get lost. Before the path was clearly marked it was necessary to take a guide. Once you have reached the great tank the rest is easy. You have only to follow the valley from the little jhil and bund. When you are looking at the ruins of the city, you should take care you do not wander away too far.

The other route, from Badarpur, is over easier country, but it is a mile longer.

You will need some food arrangements. A Hindu party might arrange to cook food at the temple dharmsala.[3] You should take your supplies with you, though there is a bazaar in Badarpur where any party could arrange for food.

---

[1] This serene landscape is miraculously unchanged.

[2] The trip could now be done in a morning (Suraj Kund is now less than 10 minutes drive from Tughlaqabad), and is particularly rewarding after the monsoon. Near Anangpur a neolithic site has been excavated (1992).

[3] This is of course no longer necessary since the establishment of the Suraj Kund tourist complex, or you could take your own picnic.

Part IV

NEW DELHI

20. THE JANTAR MANTAR[*]

The *Jantar Mantar*[1] or Delhi Observatory is in Parliament Street on the left-hand side as you go from Connaught Place to the Council House.[2] It stands in a well-kept enclosure and is maintained by the Jaipur State, to which it belongs. You will usually see the Jaipur flag flying there.[3]

The Observatory was built by the Maharajah Jai Singh of Jaipur in 1710 A.D. when Delhi was still the capital of a flourishing Mughal empire. Jai Singh was a keen astronomer who studied Hindu, Muslim and European astronomical works. He found that the astronomical tables then being used by the pandits were defective, so that the actual times of eclipses etc., were different from the times stated in the tables. He thought that this was due to the fact that the existing instruments were small and faulty. He therefore built these large instruments of his own invention. They were so solid that they could not shake, and so large that there could not be any error of calculation. Then he took observations of the stars for seven years in order to prepare a new catalogue of stars. But still Jai Singh was not quite satisfied. So he built similar observatories at Jaipur, Ujjain, Benares and Mathura.[4] Then he took observations at these places also and found that the observations in all these places fully agreed. So you see Jai Singh was a very thorough and a very patient scholar. As a result of his work

[*] The notes in this chapter have been compiled with the help of the Director of the Nehru Planetarium in New Delhi, Dr Nirupama Raghavan, to whom we are most grateful. She recommends G.R. Kaye's *Astronomical Observations of Jai Singh* for further reading.

[1] 'Jantar Mantar' is a corruption of Yantra Mantra or literally, 'Instruments and Formulae'. But it is likely that the word 'Mantar' came to be added because the phrase rolls off the tongue so trippingly (see also Jamali Kamali or various Hindi phrases such as *ulta-pulta*, topsy-turvy).

[2] The Council House is now called Sansad Bhavan or Parliament House.

[3] Since princely titles and privy purses were abolished in 1970, the former Maharajah of Jaipur no longer maintains the Delhi Jantar Mantar.

[4] The Mathura observatory is no longer there; it was reportedly broken up in the nineteenth century for the scrap value of its bricks and sold!

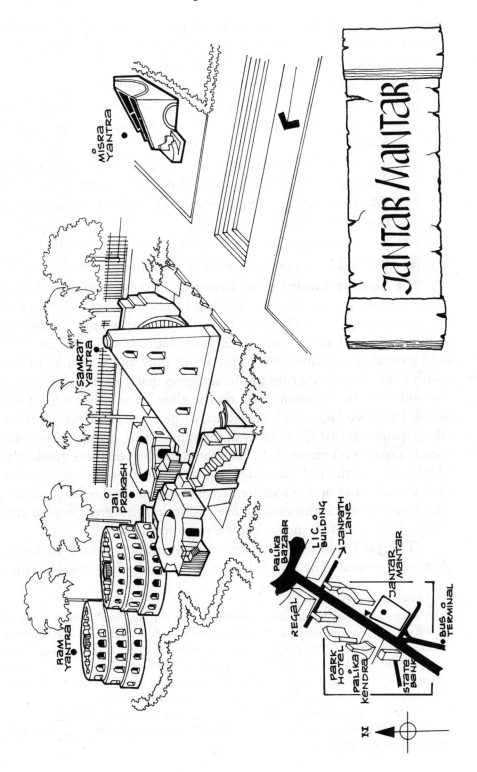

the tables used by the pandits to predict the movements of the stars were corrected. These tables have been used ever since.

The Observatory contains six instruments. They are:

(i)   *The Samrat Yantra* (The Supreme Instrument).

(ii) *The Jai Prakash* (Invention of Jai) – two complementary concave curved buildings, just to the south of the Samrat Yantra.

(iii) *The Ram Yantra* – two large circular buildings together forming a circle, to the south of the Jai Prakash.

(iv) *The Misra Yantra* (Mixed Instrument) – to the north-west of the Samrat Yantra.

(v) *A measuring platform* to the south of the Misra Yantra.

(v) *Two pillars* to the south-west of the Misra Yantra.

The **Samrat Yantra** is the largest of all the instruments. It is a huge sundial. It is what astronomers call a gnomon or a right-angled triangle standing vertically upon the earth. The hypotenuse, or sloping edge, is inclined at the same angle as the latitude of Delhi (28° 37') and so it always points towards the north pole and is parallel to the earth's axis. A staircase runs up the slope, so that you can easily climb up and read the figures marked on the edge.[1] On either side of the sundial are two large brick quadrants, or quarters of a circle. It is on these quadrants that the shadow of the sundial falls, giving us the solar or sun time.[2] You can read the time for yourselves on these quadrants. The marks on the northern edge of a quadrant show hours, minutes and seconds; and on the southern edge *gharis, pals* and *vipals*.[3] On any day you can watch the shadow moving round this great sundial and so see how the earth moves endlessly round the sun.

The **Jai Prakash** is a complicated instrument which Jai Singh himself invented. The two halves of the building form two hollows

---

[1] Now closed to visitors.

[2] The sundial markings are almost worn off now, but 'sun time' shows local time, which of course varies about an hour from east to west in India. To convert it to Indian Standard Time (GMT + 5½ hours), a corrective calculation according to the time of year must be made. IST is measured from 72.5° longitude, on a line which passes through Allahabad (the expression 'Indian Standard Time' has come to be used ironically to mean delays, as Hispanic countries refer to 'mañana'!).

0° longitude in Indian astronomical calculations passed through Ujjain.

[3] Indian astronomy divided a 60-ghari day of 24 minutes each into *pals* (24 seconds) and *vipals* (0.4 seconds).

or cups which together represent the heavenly sphere. Important points and circles are drawn on it, and in the centre there is an iron pole, with four hooks on it facing North, South, East and West. Near the bottom of the wall facing the south side of the Eastern hemisphere is a hole.[1] The sun shines through this hole only on one day in each year, 21 March, or the vernal equinox. The figures on the wall opposite show the sun's position in the heavens at the time of the equinox.

South of the Jai Prakash stands the **Ram Yantra**. It consists of two large circular buildings open at the top. Each building is a circular wall with a pillar in the middle. One building would have been sufficient, but two were built in order that spaces might be left for the observer to come in and out. Each of the two buildings is therefore not quite complete, but taken together they form one complete instrument. The purpose of the Ram Yantra[2] is to read altitude and azimuth* of the stars. This corresponds to latitude and longitude on the earth. On the walls and floors are the figures for doing this.

About 50 yards north-west of the Prakash Yantra is the **Misra Yantra** or Mixed Instrument. It is called the mixed instrument because one building contains five separate instruments. One of these is the **Niyat Chakra Yantra**. It is a sundial like the Samrat Yantra. On each side of it are two graduated semicircles. These circles represent the meridians of Greenwich (England), Zurich (Switzerland), Notkey (Japan) and Serichew (Pic Island in the Pacific). They enable us to tell the time at these places when it is noon in Delhi, and the time at Delhi when it is noon in these places. The other instruments are for various purposes. Your teachers will explain them to you.

The *two pillars* to the south-west of the Misra Yantra are built in order to determine the shortest and longest days of the year (21 December and 21 June). In December one pillar casts its shadow

---

* 'Azimuth' literally means 'vertical arc of sky from zenith to horizon – angular distance of this from the meridian'.

[1] The hole is there: the sun shines through it and falls on a specific point on the inside wall. But the wall markings are in poor condition. The chamber has seepage and is filled with garden tools and broken furniture.

[2] This is incorrect (see Spear's own footnote above). The Ram Yantra is used to measure the *altitude* and azimuth of the sun.

completely over the other pillar. In June it does not cast any shadow at all upon it.

ADDITIONAL NOTES

1. The elements of the Observatory are:
Latitude 28° 37' 35" N.
Longitude 77° 13' 5" E. of Greenwich.
Height above sea-level, 695 feet.
Local time 21 minutes 7.7 seconds after standard time.

2. The Samrat Yantra (or Supreme Instrument) is the central building of the observatory. It is built into a quadrangular excavation about 15 feet deep, 125 feet from east to west, and 120 feet from north to south. The foundation and some portion of it are below the ground level, the height now visible being 60.3 feet. It is in principle one of the simplest 'equal hour' sundials. It consists of a huge gnomon in the form of a right-angled triangle and two quadrants of a circle attached to it, one to the east and one to the west. The triangle stands in the plane of the Meridian, i.e. exactly in north-south direction. The larger side containing the right-angle measures 113.5 feet and is on the level ground while the shorter side is vertical and 60.3 feet high. The hypotenuse or the inclined edge of the gnomon is 128 feet long and is inclined to the horizontal at an angle of 28° 37' which is nearly equal to the latitude of Delhi, so that the hypotenuse points towards the north pole and is parallel to the Earth's axis.

In order to enable an observer to read graduations on the inclined edge, the gnomon is duplicated and stairs are provided between the two inclined edges. The quadrants are arcs of circles whose planes are perpendicular to the edges of the gnomon and hence parallel to the plane of the Equator, so that the shadow cast in the quadrant by the gnomon meets the edges of the quadrant at right angles. The graduations on the inclined edge[1] give declination (namely, the distance north or south of the plane of the celestial Equator). The portions of the quadrants near the points where they intersect the gnomon are now submerged under the ground and hence the local times when the sun is near the meridian on either side of it cannot be read. The width of a quadrant is 7 feet 7 inches. The graduations on the northern edge of a quadrant show hours, minutes and seconds while those on the southern edge show gharis, pals, and vipals.

On the top of the gnomon there is a small circular vertical pillar on

---

[1] Most of the markings have now worn off.

which is mounted a horizontal sundial of the European type which was probably constructed in 1910. (*N.B.* - The orifice is still there but the arc of 60° is obliterated and so the Shashthamsa Yantra is now out of order.)[1]

3. The Jai Prakash is situated immediately south of the Samrat Yantra and consists of two complementary concave hemispheres. The diameter of each hemisphere is 27 feet 5 inches. The circle forming the rim of each hemisphere is the horizon and is divided into degrees and minutes. The lowermost point in the centre represents the zenith. The two hemispheres are so constructed that some parts have been left out in each with a view to providing access to the different parts of the instrument for reading graduations, the vacant parts of one corresponding with the built parts of the other, so that the two hemispheres taken together show the complete surface of the celestial spheres and are a representation of it with the important points and circles drawn on it.[2] Originally cross-wires were stretched across each hemisphere north to south and east to west, at the point of intersection of which there was a circular piece of metal with a hole in the centre. The image of the sun passing through this hole on the concave surface indicated the position of the sun. The cross-wires are no longer there, but in the centre of the hemisphere there is now a vertical circular iron pole[3] of about 2 inches in diameter equal in height to the radius of the hemisphere and at its top four hooks facing north, east, south and west are fixed.

Near the bottom of the wall facing the south side of the eastern hemisphere there is a hole through which rays of the sun shine on a graduated arc on an inside wall of the supported chamber at one moment only in the year, namely, at the vernal equinox which occurs each year on 21 March. The graduations on the arc indicate the sun's position in the heavens at the vernal equinox.

4. The Ram Yantra is situated south of the Jai Prakash and consists of a circular wall and a circular pillar at the centre. The inside radius measured from the circumference of the central pillar to the wall is 24 feet 6 inches and the same is the height of the walls and the pillar. The diameter of the central pillar is 5 feet 3 inches. The walls and floor are graduated to read azimuth and altitude. The horizontal floor is cut up into 30 sectors at spaces of 6 degrees. The graduated sectors are supported on pillars 3 feet high so that the observer can place his eye at any point on the scale. The walls also are broken up in such a manner that one pillar of the wall is joined to one

---

[1] This room is now inaccessible to visitors.
[2] No longer fully visible.
[3] No longer there.

sector. At the sides of each opening of the walls there are notches for placing sighting bars, though there are no such bars now. The central pillar is graduated by vertical stripes each 6° in width. The two buildings could have been made only one by having the circular floor and walls continuous without leaving vacant spaces in them but to provide room for the access of the observer to all parts of the instrument, the circular floor has been divided into sectors and only alternate sectors are drawn in one building while those left out are built in the other building. Thus the vacant spaces in one correspond with the sectors in the other and vice versa.[1] The same is the case with the pillars of the circular walls. The two buildings are thus complementary, i.e. part of one and the same instrument. The use of this instrument is to find altitude and azimuth of heavenly bodies.

5. The Misra Yantra (or Mixed Instrument)[2] is situated to the north-west of Samrat Yantra at a distance of 140 feet from it. It is called the Mixed Instrument because it combines in one building five separate instruments, viz:

(i)   The Niyat. Chakra Yantra.
(ii) The Samrat Yantra.
(iii) The Agra Yantra.
(iv) The Dakshinovritti Yantra.
(v)   The Karkarasi Valaya.

(i) The Niyat Chakra Yantra occupies the middle of the building and consists of a gnomon with two graduated semi-circles on either side, ending at the central gnomon. The centres of the semi-circles lie on the gnomon, and at these centres there are holes to hold a rod or stick. The semi-circles are so constructed as to represent the meridians of Greenwich, Zurich, Notkey (a village in Japan) and Serichew (a town in Pic Island in the Pacific Ocean, east of Russia). We can therefore find the declinations of the sun at those times at Delhi which correspond to the noon at these four places, and can also find the times when it is noon at these places.

(ii) On either side of the Niyat Chakra and joined to it is half of an equinoctial dial built on the same principle as the large Samrat Yantra. The half-instrument to the west gives time and declination before noon and the other half-instrument to the east gives time and declination after noon.

[1] This can easily be seen by locating the shadow of the central pillar in both buildings. If the top of the shadow falls in the vacant space between sectors on one building, it falls on the graduated sector in the other.
[2] The Misra Yantra looks rather like a stylized 'namaste', the Indian form of greeting with palms folded together. In fact it is often reproduced to suggest greeting, and has become an Indian icon. It was built after Jai Singh's death.

(iii) The Agra Yantra (or amplitude instrument) is the second quadrant on the west side of the building. The purpose for which this was constructed in not definitely known.

(iv) The Dakshinovritti (meridian circle) is a graduated semi-circle on the eastern wall of the building and is made exactly in the North and South line, starting from 0° in the North and South to 90° in the centre. At the centre of this arc is a hole in which a peg can be fixed. It corresponds to the modern transit circle. Its use is to observe the altitude of a heavenly body when it is passing the meridian.

(v) The Karkarasi Valaya or 'circle of the sign of Cancer', is a graduated semi-circle engraved in plaster on the northern wall of the building. It is made in the east-west line, starting from 0° in the east to 180° in the west with 90° at the bottom. At the centre a peg is fixed which projects outwards from the wall towards the north. The inclination of the northern wall to the vertical is about 5°. The sun, therefore, shines over the north wall for a short period and the shadow of the centre peg falls on the graduated circle, showing the sign of the Zodiac in which the sun is passing.[1]

6. The two pillars to the south-west of the Misra Yantra distant 17 feet with the line joining their centres pointing 35° east of north determine the shortest and the longest days of the year, which occur on 21 December and 21 June respectively. In one case the southern pillar casts a full shadow on the other pillar, while in the other case it does not cast any shadow at all on it.

N.B. – To the west of the Samrat Yantra is a small building (a chowkidar's house) and on it is fixed the Jaipur Flag.

---

[1] At local noon on the summer solstice, the shadow of the peg is supposed to fall exactly on the 0 mark of the graduated circle on the wall. But now the shadow never falls on the wall. There are three possible reasons:

(i) repeated 'restorations' have altered the inclination of the north wall *and/or*

(ii) the shift of the north pole that has occurred in the two and a half centuries since the instrument was constructed has resulted in the north wall inclination becoming insufficient for the sun to shine on it at the 21 June solstice, *or*

(iii) the wall's original inclination was never sufficient to allow the sun to shine on it on 21 June. This seems unlikely as the other instruments are all highly accurate.

21. NEW DELHI

Your knowledge of Delhi will not be complete without a visit to New Delhi.[1]

New Delhi was planned by two architects – Sir Edwin Lutyens[2] and Sir Herbert Baker.[3] Sir Edwin Lutyens is now President of the Royal Academy, which is the great artistic body of England. He designed the Viceroy's House, which is the best building in New Delhi.[4] The style of the principal buildings is what we call Classical or Greek. There are pillars and domes, but with very few arches. When you find any arches you will see that they are round and not pointed. The reason why the Classical or Greek style is used in Delhi is that this style is suited to northern India.[5] Ancient Greece was a hot and dry country. The climate was rather like the climate of northern India. In summer it was not quite so hot, and the cold weather was a little colder. But in Greece the air is clear, the sky is blue and the sun usually shines.

But while the style is Classical or Greek the *details* of the buildings are Indian. For example, in the Secretariat[6] and the Viceroy's House

[1] When Spear was writing, most people still lived in what we now call Old Delhi (Shahjahanabad and Civil Lines), and New Delhi was therefore an excursion (see Afterword for more on New Delhi).

During 1931–47 the Viceroy and Government spent the winters in Delhi, but summered in Simla (except during World War II).

[2] Sir Edwin Lutyens (1869–1944), pronounced like 'much'-ins, not 'loot-yins', was President of the august Royal Academy from 1938 until his death in 1944.

[3] Sir Herbert Baker (1862–1946) was chosen by Lutyens for this project, but they later quarrelled.

[4] The Viceroy's House is now called Rashtrapati Bhavan (President's House) and, at the apex of Raj Path (formerly Kingsway), is the focus of Lutyens Delhi. See also pp. 82–3.

[5] Up to a point. The neo-classical style came most naturally to Lutyens because it was the current vogue in Britain for public buildings of all sorts, especially when building on a monumental scale as here.

[6] The Secretariat is popularly referred to as North Block or South Block.

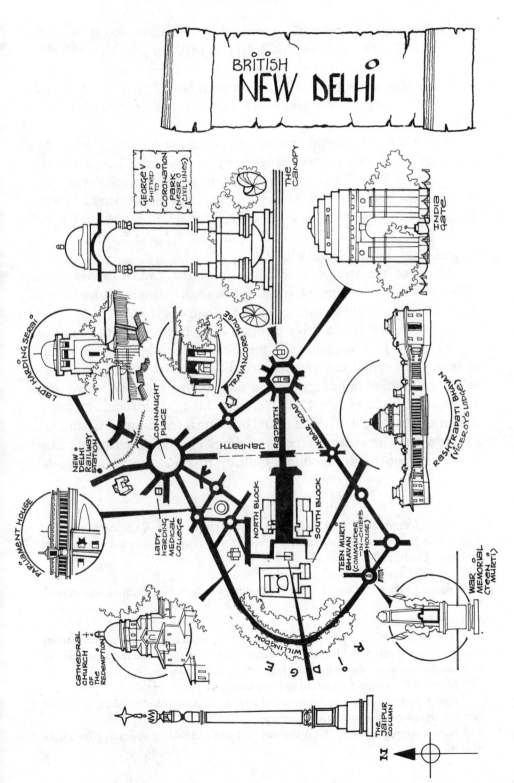

BRITISH
NEW DELHI

you will see that the columns (or pillars) are like those used at Sarnath[1]
by Asoka. There are stone and marble screens or *jalis*,[2] etc. All this
work was done by Indian masons. Some of them came from Agra
and were the descendants of the men who built Akbar's Palace[3] and
the Taj. Some came from Jaipur and some from other parts of Rajputana and India.

There is one other thing to notice about New Delhi, that is, the
planning of the city, or the arrangement of the streets. The architects
have arranged that all the main streets shall have beautiful vistas or
views at the end of them. Thus Kingsway[4] has the Viceroy's House
at one end and Purana Qila at the other. Parliament Street has a view
of the Jama Masjid,[5] and so on. You should look out for these vistas
as you drive about New Delhi.

Many of the streets have been given the names of historical
characters in the history of India. Look at the names of the streets
and see if you know anything about the names given.[6]

Now we will take a drive through New Delhi, starting from the
Ajmer Gate.[7] First we will cross the great new bridge to New Delhi
station. Just beyond this you will see the Lady Hardinge Serai.[8] This
is one of the few buildings built in the Mughal style. Then we pass
Connaught Place and the Lady Hardinge Medical College, and drive
up Parliament Street. The big round building is the Council Chamber.
Outside it is a great stone fence or railing. This is interesting because
it is a copy of the stone railings built by Asoka at the great stupa of

[1] The reference is to Asoka's column, which can be seen in the Archaeological
Museum at Sarnath, near Varanasi. Its capital of four lions was adopted as a national
emblem of independent India.

[2] See p. 37 for more on *jali* fretwork.

[3] 'Akbar's Palace' can mean either the buildings in Agra Fort or those in Fatehpur
Sikri.

[4] See p. 94, note 4.

[5] The Jama Masjid cannot be seen clearly from Sansad Marg (Parliament Street)
because of intervening buildings, but you can see it quite well from the north side of
Connaught Circus on the radial road between C and D block.

[6] Many of the original names have been changed.

[7] Ajmeri Gate is today a very congested area, not a good place to start a drive, but
you can follow Spear's route from our map.

[8] Now a women's hostel, this is the dark red domed building opposite New Delhi
Station.

Sanchi, near Bhopal. If the Assembly is not sitting you can go[1] inside and see the Assembly Chamber, the Council of State and the Chamber of Princes. The internal decoration is very fine. Notice the stone lamp-posts outside the building. These are copies of Mughal lamps at Agra.[2]

Next we come to the great open space outside the Secretariat.[3] On the Secretariat buildings you will see chhattris in the Mughal style. There are also carved elephants and bell ornaments, which are copied from Hindu architecture. In the space between the two Secretariat buildings are columns which have gilt ships on the tops. These represent the different Dominions of the British Empire. You should walk through the corridors of the Secretariat and see the courtyards inside.[4] The Secretariat was designed by Sir Herbert Baker.

In front of you is now the Viceroy's House. It is the best proportioned building in New Delhi. The dome is specially fine. In front is the column presented by the Maharajah of Jaipur. On the top of it is the Star of India.[5] Behind the house is a beautiful Mughal garden.[6]

From the Viceroy's House we will drive back to Connaught Place. Turn left by the Regal Cinema and drive right round the Willingdon

---

[1] The Council Chamber is now Sansad Bhavan (Parliament House), which contains the Lok Sabha (People's House) and Rajya Sabha (States' House). Indian nationals can obtain a visitor's pass by application to the Parliamentary Secretariat, in a building next to Sansad Bhavan. Foreign nationals should apply through their Embassy or High Commission. Visitors should note that parking is restricted and it is advisable to arrive by taxi.

[2] The lamp-posts outside the Taj Mahal are made of metal.

[3] 'The great open space' is the Vijay Chowk (Victory Place), where the annual Beating Retreat ceremony takes place on 29 January each year.

[4] The gilt ships look quite black now. The North Block courtyard is open to the public: the walls are inscribed with princely state emblems and quotations from Queen Victoria's 1858 proclamation.

[5] Designed by Lutyens, the Jaipur column is in the tradition of commemorative pillars, 'replete with Indian and imperial allegories' (Irving, p. 247) and surmounted by a glass Star of India. This was a copy of the decoration of the Order of the Star of India (1861), but with *six* points instead of five.

[6] Viceroy Hardinge, after a visit to Kashmir, was eager for a 'Mughal' garden. This garden is 'Mughal' as seen by a man famous for the very English gardens he created with Gertrude Jekyll. It is open to the public each February (N.B. Photography is not allowed).

Crescent.[1] At first the road goes straight. Near the end of the straight is the Talkatora Garden.[2] You will see that part of this is a Mughal garden. Just here the Marathas fought a battle with the Mughals in 1738. Two Mughal armies were near Agra, but the Marathas stepped between them, rode 120 miles in two days and plundered the fair at Kalka Devi near Okhla. The young nobles went out to meet them. But they were defeated at Talkatora. This is the first time that the Marathas came to Delhi.

The Willingdon Crescent goes right round the Viceroy's House. You have a fine view of the house all the way. When we have got right round we come to the Commander-in-Chief's House. Outside it is the War Memorial to the Indian Army.[3] Then we will drive down Aurangzeb Road till it joins Prithviraj Road. This leads us to the great War Memorial Arch. Round this space the Princes are building their palaces. The chief ones are those of Hyderabad, Baroda, Bikaner, Jaipur and Patiala.[4] A little way along Curzon Road is the Travancore Palace. It is not very large, but is one of the most beautiful.[5]

We will return along Hardinge Avenue and under the railway bridge. Just beyond on the right is the mosque and tomb of Sheikh Abdun Nabi. He was one of Akbar's orthodox opponents. He went

[1] Willingdon Crescent escaped the post-1947 re-naming of streets and buildings with British names.

[2] Once a walled tank, Tal (tank) Katora (cup) is now a garden, and a stadium.

[3] Built as the Commander-in-Chief's house, on a prime site with a direct vista on to the Viceroy's House, it was renamed Teen Murti Bhavan after 1947 and became Jawaharlal Nehru's residence as Prime Minister. It now houses the Nehru Memorial Museum, Planetarium, a library of modern history and an auditorium. There is another of Firoz Shah's Kushk-i-shikars in the grounds, opposite the Planetarium. The War Memorial is the Teen Murti (Three Statues) in the centre of the roundabout outside, commemorating those in the princely cavalry regiments of Hyderabad, Jodhpur and Mysore killed in the 1914–18 war.

[4] Lutyens built Hyderabad House (now used for official functions) and Baroda House (now the headquarters of the Northern Railway). Bikaner House is the Rajasthan Tourism office and Jaipur House is the National Gallery of Modern Art; Patiala House is now part of the Delhi law courts.

[5] Curzon Road is now called Kasturba Gandhi Marg after Mahatma Gandhi's wife, and Travancore House is still there for the moment, though it was announced in the press in April 1993 that it was to be torn down to make way for another multi-storey building.

to Mecca, and while there he heard of the rebellion of Akbar's brother, Mohammed Hakim. He was so pleased that he returned at once to join in it. But when he arrived in Sind the rebellion was finished and he was taken prisoner by Akbar. Soon after a mob burst into his prison and killed him. So even this old building has an exciting history.[1]

ADDITIONAL NOTES

The Assembly. A visit to the Legislative Assembly when it is in session will be interesting and instructive. Your teacher can get tickets from any member of the Assembly. Notice the President in his wig,[2] like the Speaker of the House of Commons, and also how the Government members sit on his right hand and the Opposition on the left. You should go early because the public galleries are usually crowded.

The Viceroy's House. Permission to visit the Viceroy's House can sometimes be obtained when the Viceroy is not in residence. The best parts of the House are:

1. The circular **Throne Room**, where Investitures and Durbars take place.[3]
2. The **Ballroom**. Notice specially the ceilings. The painting in the centre is of Fateh Ali Shah of Persia, and the Mughal style decoration is by Italian artists.[4]
3. The **Banqueting Hall**. Here is the Viceregal gold and silver plate. Round the walls are pictures of many of the Governors-General and Viceroys. It will make people feel more real to you if you can see their pictures.[5]

---

[1] This is at the intersection of Bahadurshah Zafar Marg and the road leading east to the I.T.O. bridge. A well-designed community hall and library, faced with Delhi quartz to match the mosque, was built next to the mosque in the 1990s.

[2] Wigs, like *sola topis* (pith helmets), went out with the British Raj!

[3] The Throne Room is now called the Durbar Hall.

[4] No. The work was done by Indian artists under the supervision of Percy Brown, the art historian. The Ball Room is now called the Ashoka Hall.

[5] The portraits were taken down after Independence, but in 1992 many were retrieved from storage and arranged for display in the large ground floor Marble Room. The Banqueting Hall is now called the State Dining Room.

The Museum. This is in Queensway[1] just beyond the point where it crosses Kingsway. It is worth a visit by itself. Here you will find a wonderful collection of paintings brought back by Sir Aurel Stein[2] from the buried cities in Central Asia. They date from the 1st to the 6th century A.D. and they show how Indian influence had spread with Buddhism right into Central Asia. The Curator will be very glad to show you round and explain everything.

In the Record Office[3] nearby is another part of the Museum where there is a fine collection of Tibetan banners and other objects. The full name of this Museum is the Museum of Central Asian Antiquities.

---

[1] This museum was a small building which was replaced in 1955–60 by the present National Museum, built on the same site in Janpath (formerly Queensway).

[2] Sir Aurel Stein (1862–1943) was born in Austria. He became principal of the Oriental College in Lahore and undertook many geographical and archaeological expeditions to Kashmir, Iran and Central Asia as well as scholarly research on Sanskrit.

[3] Now called the National Archives of India. Intended as one of four public buildings at the corners of the road-crossing, it was designed by Lutyens, with the addition of a large extension in the 1980s.

Part V

THE ARCHITECTURE OF DELHI

22. THE ARCHITECTURE OF DELHI

I. HINDU ARCHITECTURE

Before the Muslims came to Delhi the Hindus built their temples in what we now call the Jain style of northern India. The finest temples of this style which still exist are the Jain temples at Mount Abu in Rajputana. They are all built of marble and are very beautiful indeed. You can see all that survives of this style in Delhi in the court of the great Qutb mosque. The pillars of this court were taken from temples by Qutbuddin Aibak and used for this new mosque.

The special thing to notice is that the Hindus of those days did *not use the arch*. They used square pillars to support the roofs of their buildings. They did not build domes either, Instead they laid one stone over another until they met in the middle as Fig. 8. On the pillars they carved the figures of gods. They also carved various ornaments, such as temple bells, flowers and trees. The carving of flowers

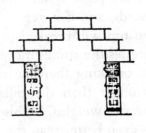

FIG. 8

and trees is called *naturalistic* because it is an imitation of nature. This is what the Muslims found when they captured Delhi in 1192 A.D.

II. THE SLAVE KINGS[1]

When Qutbuddin Aibak came to Delhi, the first thing he wanted to do was to build a mosque. And of course he wanted to build the same sort of mosque that he knew in his own land of Ghor (modern Afghanistan). Now the architects of Ghor liked *pointed arches and domes*

---

[1] The Il-bari Turks.

and they wanted to have them in Delhi. But the Hindu workmen had never used arches and their own builders were far away.[1]

The Arch

Let us understand the principle and use of the arch. The arch consists of a number of stones so cut and arranged that they form the circumference of a circle whose centre is the centre of the arch.

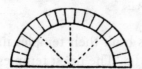

FIG. 9

Thus the centre stone of the arch is called the keystone, because it is that stone which holds the arch together. It does not matter whether the arch is pointed or round, the principle is the same.

The *use* of the arch is that it will carry much bigger weights than pillars supporting horizontal slabs like Fig. 10. In the pillar system the weight presses downwards, and if it gets very heavy the stone slab on top will break. But the weight on an arch presses the stones more firmly together instead of breaking them apart. So the arch is much stronger than the pillar and will bear much heavier weights. In this respect the pointed arch is even better than the round arch.

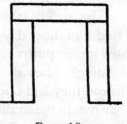

FIG. 10

The Romans liked the round arch, but the Arabs liked the pointed arch. The first Arab building with pointed arches was the mosque of Samarra in Iraq, built in 752 A.D. After that all Muslims used the pointed arch and also the Europeans in the Middle Ages. The European style of pointed arches is called the Gothic style.

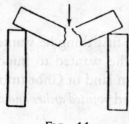

FIG. 11

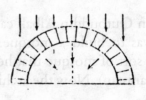

FIG. 12

[1] No. The Indians had used trabeated arches. These continued to be built, along with arcuated structures well into the Mughal period.

So we have in Delhi kings who wanted arches and builders who did not know about them. The result is the *style of the Slave Kings*.

In this style you will find that pillars are used for the main mosque building and at the west end are large sham arches. We call these arches sham because they do not possess a keystone. They are just *cut* to look like arches. You can tell a true from a sham arch in this way. A true arch is one whose stones are cut so that they would

FIG. 13

meet in the centre of the arch. A sham arch is one whose stones are cut quite straight and point to the ground like Fig. 13.

Examples:

The arches of the great Qutb mosque.

Sultan Ghari's tomb

Arhai-din-ki-Jhompra mosque, Ajmer.

The next thing to notice is that the Muslims did not allow any representation of living things on their buildings. But the Hindu workmen were still allowed to carve flowers and trees. You will see this naturalistic carving on the pillars of the arches of the Qutb mosque. The Arabic texts are almost smothered by this carving.

Iltutmish brought craftsmen from Ghor, who introduced the decorative patterns of the Muslim world. They are called geometrical or formal, because they are like the figures of geometry and have no resemblance to living nature.

Examples:

The first is on the arches of Iltutmish's extension of the Qutb mosque. The next is on Iltutmish's tomb close by.

The Khiljis

As time went on more workmen came and introduced the knowledge of the true arch. This is the special feature of the buildings of Alauddin Khilji. He used the true arch and he used the geometrical pattern. He also used a dome.[1] The principle of the dome is that of the true arch applied to a roof. So now we have the first Muslim style complete. Its marks are: (i) the arch instead of the pillar; (ii) the dome

[1] 'The dome of an Islamic building is a representation of the vault of heaven, for Quranic law requires that Muslims be buried under the open sky' (Goodall).

instead of a flat roof or the *shikhara*; (iii) geometrical instead of naturalistic designs for carving.

Examples:

The Alai Darwaza at the Qutb.

The Jama'at Khana Mosque at Nizamuddin.

Both these buildings are very fine.

III. THE TUGHLAQS

We have seen how the Slave and Khilji kings gradually got rid of all the specially Hindu features in their buildings. Now we shall see how they were brought back again, and used to form a truly Indian style of architecture. The Tughlaq kings had a very special style of their own.

Firstly, it was very simple and had very little ornamentation. The materials they used were plain stone covered with plaster instead of the rich red stone of the Khiljis and the Mughals. For the reason of this see Chapter 5.

Secondly, their buildings were very strong and solid. They often had sloping walls, and remind us of the great buildings of Egypt. They all make us think of fortresses, even if it is a mosque or college at which we are looking. In this they reflect the spirit of the times, because Hindustan was through all these years threatened by the wild Mongols who had destroyed the civilization of Iran.

Thirdly, the Tughlaq buildings are all very well proportioned. They give us the impression that their shape is just right, neither too much nor too little.

Fourthly, they use in their buildings Hindu features. One of these is the square pillar supporting a roof or sometimes a doorway. Another is the lotus ornament. There are many Tughlaq buildings in Delhi. Here are some examples of each of these four points:

(i)   Firoz Shah Kotla, Firoz Shah's tomb at the Hauz Khas.

(ii) Tughlaqabad, Ghiyasuddin Tughlaq's tomb.

(iii) Any of the Tughlaq buildings illustrate this, but note specially Ghiyasuddin's tomb, Firoz Shah's tomb and the mosque at Firoz Shah Kotla.

(iv) The madarsa at the Hauz Khas.

IV. THE FIFTEENTH CENTURY

Sayyids and Lodis

The style of the fifteenth century is a continuation of the previous Tughlaq style. There was still a shortage of money, so that the expensive materials of the Khiljis and the Mughals could not be used. But there was development in design and increasing fusion of Hindu and Muslim elements to form a genuine Indian style. This process reached its furthest point in the buildings of Sher Shah. Let us now notice the chief of these developments.

The Tomb

The earlier tomb was a square building with a dome on the top. In the fifteenth century, however, the square became an octagon. Round the tomb was built a verandah. This verandah was supported by square pillars in the Hindu style. The dome was now placed on a drum, or circular piece of masonry like Fig 14. The domes were at first *flat* or half-domes, but later in the century, as the builders became more skilled, they became larger, until they

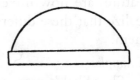

FIG. 14

became complete semi-circles, or full domes. The first full dome in Delhi is that of the Bara Gumbad in the Willingdon Park.[1] The top of the dome was always surmounted by the lotus. There was a space round the dome, on the roof of the verandah. This space was filled up by chhattris, one on each of the eight sides of the dome. These chhattris also had Hindu pillars. The purpose of these chhattris was to hide the drum from view, and the purpose of the drum was to make the dome higher. The impression we receive is that of a cluster of domes around the great central dome. Inside, the walls were plastered, decorated with Arabic texts and painted in various colours.

Examples:

The tombs of Mubarak Shah Sayyid and Sikandar Lodi in the Willingdon Park.

The nameless tomb at Khairpur near the Moth-ki-Masjid.

---

[1] Now called Lodi Garden.

Isa Khan's tomb near Humayun's tomb.
The finest of all these tombs is Sher Shah's tomb at Sasseram, near Gaya, Bihar.

The Mosque

The mosques had no minarets. The call to prayer was given from the roof. But at the back corners of the mosque were placed little towers. These have sloping, rounded sides and are in five stages. Look at them carefully and you will see that they are models of the Qutb Minar. This feature is peculiar to Delhi and to the fifteenth century. An example of this is the Bara Gumbad mosque in the Willingdon Park.

The finest buildings of this period are those of Sher Shah. They are the finest, firstly, because they have the best proportions; secondly, because in them are blended different coloured stones which form a beautiful colour scheme, and thirdly, because the Hindu and Muslim features are now mixed together in perfect harmony. You will not realize that these different features exist unless you specially look for them.

Examples:

Sher Shah's mosque in the Purana Qila.

The Moth-ki-Masjid.

The gateway of the Purana Qila.

V. The Mughals

The Mughal style really began with the return of Humayun to Delhi in 1555. The first thing which strikes us is that their buildings are much more magnificent than the previous ones. They are much larger, and red stone and marble are freely used. This is because the Mughal emperors were far more powerful and richer than the Sayyids and Lodis. They had fewer enemies than the Tughlaqs or Khiljis, and so had more money to spend on buildings. Most of the Mughal emperors were men of great taste and judgement. So they chose their architects or *ustaads* well, with the idea of enriching with beauty not only India, but the whole world.

The Garden

The Mughals brought some new ideas from Iran. One of these was the use of beautiful blue tiles on their domes.[1] You can see some of these on the tomb in the middle of the main road opposite Humayun's tomb. Another was the formal or geometrical garden. In Iran, which is hilly, these gardens were arranged in seven terraces, representing the seven stages of Paradise. Water ran down the centre of these gardens. The Mughals loved running water, because in Afghanistan and Iran water and rain are scarce, and you can only have a garden where there is a spring of water. Sometimes they built pleasure gardens only. The Shalimar gardens at Lahore and Srinagar are still in working order. They also always enclosed their tombs in gardens. The tomb was a pleasure house until the death of the owner, and then his descendants used pavilions at the side of the garden. You can see how a tomb garden was laid out at Humayun's tomb and Safdarjang's tomb. At Safdarjang's tomb you can see the pavilions used by visitors after his death.

The Tomb

The Mughal tomb differed from the previous ones in several ways. It was square[2] instead of octagonal, and it had no verandahs. Above all, it was placed on a large stone platform. The dome was a complete semi-circle and was placed on a high drum. At first the dome had no lotus on it, only a metal crescent (as in Humayun's tomb), but later they went back to the lotus. At each corner of the tomb was a chhattri. The drum was hidden by a great darwaza or doorway on each side of the tomb. You can see all these things for yourself when you visit Humayun's tomb. The dome was of white marble and the building of red stone.

As time went on the dome became more than a semicircle, that is to say, bulbous, like Fig. 15.[3] You can tell the date of a Mughal

[1] In fact ceramic tiles (chiefly blue and green), though *first* used in Iran and Central Asia, were introduced into India before the Mughals, at the time of the Lodis, e.g. Shish Gumbad in Lodi Gardens and Moth-ki-Masjid.

[2] Some of the Lodi tombs were also square.

[3] Ali Mardan Khan (see p. 10) is 'believed to have introduced the bulbous Tartar dome into Indian architecture' (see Beale).

tomb roughly by two tests. The later the date
of the tomb, the more bulbous is the dome,
and the poorer is the material employed.
Compare in this respect Humayun's tomb
with Safdarjang's tomb.

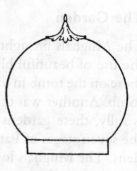

FIG. 15

Sometimes the Mughals added minarets
to their tombs. You can see how this
developed in Akbar's tomb at Sikandra,
Agra, in Jehangir's tomb at Lahore, and in
the Taj Mahal. But most of the tombs had
no minarets.

Examples:
   Humayun's tomb.
   Abdur Rahim Khan-e-Khanan's tomb.[1]
   Atgah Khan's tomb.
   Safdarjang's tomb.

The Mosque

The Mughals of course followed the usual plan of all mosques. But
they added some special features of their own. The first was the
minaret. The minaret was borrowed from Persia,[2] and there were
usually two of them. The Jama Masjid has two, but none of the earlier
Jama Masjids had any. Remember that the Qutb Minar was probably
a Tower of Victory, not an ordinary minaret.

The second development was in the domes. These were placed
on drums and were bulbous in shape. The later the date of the mosque,
the more bulbous the dome. The domes were of white marble. But

---

[1] This is on the eastern side of the Mathura road. Abdur Rahim 'Khan-e-Khanan'
(Chief of Chiefs — 1556–1626) was a senior official of Akbar's court, who rose to
become Commander-in-Chief. He was a generous patron of the arts, a gifted linguist
and translator, whose Hindi verses are popular throughout north India.

[2] During the Seljuq period (1038–1157) the new cylindrical minaret form appeared
(see Michell, *Art of the Islamic World*, p. 251). The Seljuqs were Central Asian nomads
who conquered the area from Syria to Afghanistan and rose to power with a mixture
of Persian administrative skill and Turkish military ability.

they also had thin strips of black marble running down them. The later the date the thicker are these strips. Compare the dome of the Jama Masjid with those of the Zinat-ul-Masajid, Daryaganj, which was built sixty years later.

As with the tombs, in later days (from 1700 onwards) the mosques deteriorated. The domes became more bulbous. The strips in the domes became larger, and the proportions of the buildings were not so good. Above all the materials used were inferior. This was because there was less money. The many wars prevented much building and so good architects were not encouraged and took up other occupations. Compare the Jama Masjid with the Sonehri Masjid outside the Fort (1754) or with the mosque at Safdarjang's Tomb.

Examples:

The Jama Masjid.

The Fatehpuri Masjid

The Zinat-ul-Masajid

The Anglo-Arabic College mosque.

AFTERWORD – FIFTY YEARS ON

Laura Sykes

As you drive through the streets of Delhi, try counting the number of objects you can see which would also have been there, in more or less identical form, 50, 100, or even 500 years ago. Although there is no danger of the pedestrian or passenger on Aurobindo Marg, say, forgetting he is living in the late twentieth century, the tally is surprising: cows, stray dogs and monkeys; occasionally elephants and performing bears, donkeys and camels; street vendors of sugarcane juice, *paan* and *chaat*; men sitting around on *charpoys* or *muras* at roadside food stalls; earthen water pots of cool drinking water left for thirsty passers-by; and so on.

The city has changed enormously in the last fifty years, making it difficult for its would-be explorers to search out all the monuments with only the first edition of Spear's book, but this updated and annotated, illustrated and indexed version aims to simplify the search, and entertain you on the way.

What would it have been like, for example, to be a citizen of Firoz Shah's Delhi? Or of Shahjahan's? The historical figures Spear wrote about were as real to him as his next door neighbours, and as he went through the streets of Delhi it is obvious from the way he writes that he was visualizing Timur coming in the opposite direction with his 'Mongol hordes', or Shahjahan and Ali Mardan discussing their next building project. If you can enter his world of historical fantasy (as Khushwant Singh did to write *his Delhi*) you too will discover a haunted and haunting city, which still has the remains of a fascinating past to reveal to those prepared to dig just a little below the late twentieth-century surface; in fact its ghosts will assail you at the most unexpected moments.

Spear has explained so vividly how Delhi's architectural features have developed over the centuries, its arches and domes in particular, that it is worth trying to visit the various cities in the order that they were built; the notes that follow therefore describe those cities where there is anything to add to Spear's account in *chronological* order, rather than in Spear's. The * after the heading indicate the historical and architectural significance of the site, along the lines of *Michelin* guides (* = worth going to see, ** = worth making an effort to see, *** = worth coming to India just to see!); ♥ symbols indicate the charm and atmosphere of the site – in my subjective judgement. (Please feel free to disagree!)

After all, the magnetism of India in general and Delhi in particular has drawn tourists and conquerors for many centuries. At least one potential invader was a woman, as Jan Morris relates:

> Ibn Batuta, the best travelled man in the world, describes the country of Tawalisi, a place otherwise unknown to geography, in which he met a princess of warlike tastes, who commanded a corps of Amazons and often engaged in single combat herself. This fierce lady, who was Governor of Kaylakari, was much taken by Ibn Batuta's descriptions of India, and decided she would like to conquer that country. 'I must', she drawled, 'positively make an expedition to it, and take possession of it myself, for the quantity of its riches and its troops attracts me'. Ibn Batuta had been on the road for twenty years, and knew all about women. 'Do so', he simply replied, and left it at that .

But first, why is Delhi where it is? Various suggestions have been put forward. John Finnemore's is perhaps the most poetic:

> Age by age, invader after invader has swept into the land through the Khyber pass, that solitary gap in the vast mountain rampart, the only path by which India may be entered. All have marched down from the hills and entered with delight the rich plains of the Punjab. Then, upon gaining them, they have heard with wonder stories of a fairer and more goodly land to the south east, a land of splendid cities stored with wealth, of broad plains waving with luxuriant crops, a land of corn and wine and oil. So they pushed on and on. On their right hand they found a vast desert spreading away. On their left rose the vast mountain wall of the Himalaya. But straight ahead an easy way lay before them. . . . Not only did the plains of old Delhi offer an easy way, it also afforded ample stores of food. So from the earliest days every invader had to seize Delhi and hold Delhi. To seize it that he might be able to march forward, to hold it lest he should find his road barred on the way back. To do this he had to be the strongest man of his day. Therefore he who held Delhi, held India.

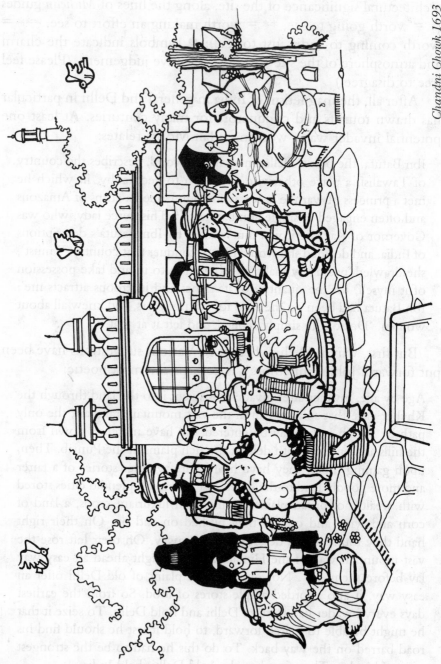

Chandni Chowk 1693

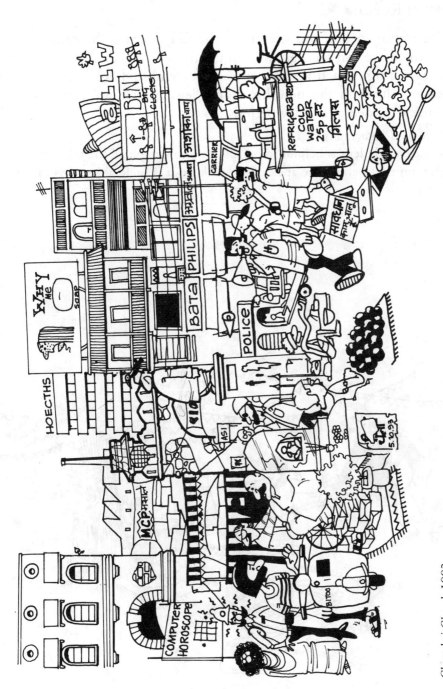

Chandni Chowk 1993

SURAJ KUND ✳ ♥

The importance of this site lies in the fact that it is the earliest city of which we can see significant building remains, but its charm lies in its setting, which is still relatively peaceful mid-week and out of season, although the new hotel and 'leisure facilities' can make it rather crowded at holiday periods.

Note on Photography
A wide-angle lens is helpful to be able to photograph all the tank at once. The sun rises behind the apex of the tank, so it is preferable to visit in the late afternoon.

Suraj Kund Mela

THE QUTB MINAR *** ♥♥♥

The monuments around the Qutb Minar span thirteen hundred years. As Spear suggests, why not begin with the oldest artefact on the site, the iron pillar, and follow with each successive building in the order that they were built, so you can visualize what the whole area must have looked like at each stage.

According to its Sanskrit inscription, the iron pillar was a *dhvaja* (standard) of Vishnu dating from the fourth–fifth century, erected by Chandragupta on a hill called Vishnupada (probably in Bihar). It was brought to Delhi – the area then called Lal Kot – by the Tomar king Anang Pal in 1052. Although spoilsport sticklers for accuracy insist that the pillar extends only 93 cm below ground, according to legend it was in fact driven down deep into the earth until firmly anchored in one of the thousand heads of Shesh Nag, the king of serpents who forms Vishnu's couch when he sleeps between incarnations. Not knowing when to leave well alone, and despite terrible warnings of doom from the priests, Anang Pal then insisted on pulling the pillar up again to make sure it had been well and truly embedded in the first place. The pillar was indeed smeared with the blood of the serpent

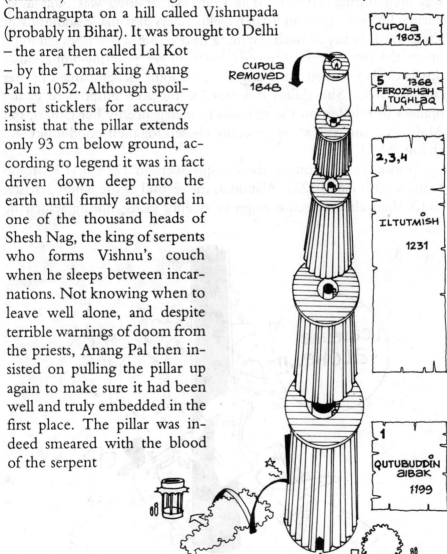

The Building of the Qutb Minar

king, but Anang Pal's failure to take this on trust was to lead to the fall of his '*Dilli*' (loose) dynasty (Sleeman). Every tourist knows the other legend associated with the pillar: stand with your back against it, and if you can join your hands behind you, your dearest wish will come true. As only the most supple can perform this gymnastic feat, which needs india-rubber limbs, it is perhaps on this account that yoga is so popular in India.

The mosque (Quwwat-ul-Islam Masjid) in which the pillar stands was built during 1191-97. The Qutb Minar itself was built next, during 1200–20 (although later Delhi rulers also made additions or alterations). Emily Metcalfe, writing in the 1880s, describes climbing up to the top of this elongated index finger pointing imperiously skywards, bejewelled with rings at each joint, accompanied by her father's ADC. She claims this was for the sole purpose of eating oranges (forbidden on the grounds of inelegance by her father), but ADCs in those days were generally chosen for their good looks and charm (M.M. Kaye).

Iltutmish's additions to the mosque were in 1225, and his tomb to the west is dated 1238. Alauddin, the second of the Khilji dynasty, had a then almost record reign of twenty years, during which he

The Iron Pillar

doubled the size of the mosque, built the celebrated Alai Darwaza (1310), founded a *madarsa*, and began the Alai Minar (1311–15), grandiosely intended to be twice the size of the Qutb Minar, but Alauddin died before completing the first storey. His tomb (1315) is on the south side of the enclosure, opposite Iltutmish's. It is customary at this point in guide books to offer some pious comment such as 'Man proposes, God disposes', but in fact there is an irony of history hidden here. Qutbuddin also only completed the first storey of *his* minar, yet subsequent rulers made a point of adding another tier or repairing it until today's awe-inspiring tower was arrived at. The Alai Minar, on the other hand, was left to languish. Was this a judgement on aesthetic grounds? Or of the relative historical importance of the two men? Probably the latter; everyone wants to be associated with a success and, although Alauddin was an important consolidator, it was Qutbuddin who established the city and the dynasty.

Just to the east of the Alai Darwaza is the delicately pretty pavilion tomb of Imam-i-Zamin (1539), and northwest of that again is Major Smith's cupola, a sort of Mughal *chhattri*. Major Smith was one of the many Army engineers who constructed government buildings across British India, usually adapted from plans of British neo-classical buildings, but the decision to add a *Mughal* finishing touch, perfectly acceptable to his eighteenth-century contemporaries, steeped in the Europeans' prevailing fondness for the *Oriental* and the *Picturesque*, did not find favour with the more scholarly antiquarian approach of the nineteenth century Lord Hardinge, who objected to it as an anachronism. It now fulfils quite happily the rôle of 'folly' in this otherwise empty part of the gardens.

Note on Photography
The Qutb Minar can be photographed at any time of day, depending on the angle you choose to take it from. In the morning, an unusual view can be had from Major Smith's cupola, looking past the Alai Darwaza, and this is the best time to take Iltutmish's screen in the mosque. In the evening, looking back through the other side of Iltutmish's screen, you can frame the more usual view of the Minar.

SIRI * ♥

While all this building was going on, the Mongols were making increasingly frequent raids on the city of Lal Kot. In 1303 Alauddin decided to face the raiders, and set up camp on the plains of Siri. However, after two months of siege, the Mongols inexplicably went away, just when they were on the point of winning. Spear's explanation (p. 54) is that the Mongols did not like the heat and were not strong enough to storm the walls, but a contemporary chronicler records:

> The Mongols came up on every side [but] by the mercy of God the Mongol was unable to find any means of forcing the camp and overpowering the royal army. After two months, the powers of the wretched prevailed and the accursed Taghi retreated towards his own country. The . . . preservation of Delhi seemed, to wise men, one of the wonders of the age. The Mongols had sufficient force to take it; they arrived at the most opportune time, they made themselves masters of the roads, and hemmed in the royal army and its appurtenances. The Sultan's army had not been replenished, and no reinforcements reached it (Z .Barni).

Delhi's escape has also been ascribed to the prayers of the Chisti saint Nizamuddin and it is suggested that Alauddin later built the Jama'at Khana mosque next to the Nizamuddin dargah in grateful thanks (Russell and Islam). Alauddin now moved his capital here and, at the same time, built the tank at neighbouring Hauz Khas to ensure the city's water supply. Ibn Batuta, writing in 1325, describes him as a benevolent ruler:

> He used to investigate the conditions of his subjects in person, and to enquire into the prices which they had to pay, and he used to send for the *muhtasib* (inspector of markets), whom they call the *rais*, every day for that purpose.

Keeping down the rate of inflation is of course one of the chief factors by which we judge the success of a government even now!

TUGHLAQABAD ** ♥♥♥

Although there is much less to see here than at, say, Shahjahan's Lal Qila, Tughlaqabad is a place where you can wander virtually alone in the almost lunar landscape and allow your imagination free rein. Let the walls themselves tell you their story in the welcome stillness: for once no one will try to sell you postcards and there's not a snake-charmer in sight.

You now enter it from a small opening on the southeast, but the original approach was by a gentle gradient from the northwest. It is named after Ghiyasuddin Tughlaq who, according to Ibn Batuta, once suggested to 'a former sultan': 'O master of the world, it were fitting that a city should be built here.' This former ruler's deceptively simple reply was 'When you are Sultan, build it.' Ghiyasuddin *did* come to power as the first of the Tughlaq dynasty (1320–1415), and within two years had built mosques, palaces and houses behind a walled perimeter 7 miles long and of a massive thickness. There are deep water storage tanks, and subterranean passages said to lead to the village outside. Marvelling at the immense size of the construction, a nineteenth-century tourist asked a passing Gujar how on earth it was built. To the Gujar there was no mystery and he gave the plausible – if pithy – reply: *'Paise, paise, paise'* ! (Boileau)

Nizamuddin comes into the story again at this point. Throughout his long life, Nizamuddin's relationship with the rulers of Delhi was rather like that of Merlin at Camelot: he was a powerful ally, but a dangerous man to cross. Either forgetting or choosing to ignore this, Ghiyasuddin requisitioned for Tughlaqabad the workmen excavating the tank at Nizamuddin's dargah. When Nizamuddin arranged for

The Rhesus Monkeys at Tughlaqabad

the builders to work for him at night, Ghiyasuddin forbade the sale of oil (for lamps) to him. Nizamuddin miraculously turned the water of the tank to oil, but cursed Tughlaqabad: *'Ya base Gujar, Ya rahe ujar'* (May it be inhabited by herdsmen or remain desolate); the point of the curse was that Gujars are nomadic, and Nizamuddin really meant that Tughlaqabad would never be a settled centre of population, an important pre-condition for Islam to prosper. In 1325, only five years after its construction, the city was indeed abandoned on the death of Ghiyasuddin, probably for lack of water as Spear suggests (even powerful curses need practical help from geology).

South-east across the road from the city walls is Ghiyasuddin's tomb. Nikhat Qaiyum recently wrote about the somewhat ambivalent Islamic attitude to mausoleums:

> Traditional Islam has developed to a remarkable degree the arts associated with death. And strangely, although there are numerous monumental tombs, Islamic disapproval of them has also been quite deep-rooted. . . . Tombs, as a symbolic expression of authority and power, constitute a deliberate display of personal and dynastic worldly achievements. Many of them, like the tomb of [Ghiyasuddin] Tughlaq, were focal points in the layout of cities . . . Human vanities and ambitions often prevailed over the strictures of faith, however orthodox and rigid they might be. The architecture of death expresses the need for the symbolic attainment of immortality.

Ghiyasuddin's is a perfectly preserved example of the familiar mixture of red sandstone and marble, but could not be more different in mood from, say, Safdarjang's delicate tomb, built four hundred years later. In European terms it is Norman or Romanesque, though actually contemporary with the Gothic period. With sloping walls like an Egyptian pyramid, which it also resembles in solidity if not in size, Ghiyasuddin's rugged tomb even now exudes the imperial grandeur of this warrior-king. The tomb also acted as a look-out fort, as can be seen from the bifocal arrow slits, i.e. long-distance vantage points alternate with close-up views of the ground immediately below the fortress. Apparently impervious to the awe-inspiring atmosphere, myriads of apple-green parakeets provide a welcome touch of levity, nesting cheekily in its perforated walls.

Ghiyasuddin was to lie in the tomb sooner than he expected. His imminent return from war in Bengal frightened Nizamuddin's followers, who daily warned him of Ghiyasuddin's approach. Nizamuddin, who had prophesied that Ghiyasuddin would never return to Delhi after these wars, remained unperturbed: *'Dilli hanoz dur ast'*, he repeated: 'Delhi is yet far off'. Sure enough, the pavilion built by Mohammed Tughlaq, the heir apparent, to welcome his father home after victory in battle, collapsed as Ghiyasuddin entered and killed him. Surprisingly, you might think, the dutiful son Mohammed Tughlaq was not in the pavilion at the time. Based on this damning circumstantial evidence, detective historians have retrospectively found him guilty of parricide.

Note on Photography
If you take the right-hand turning for Suraj Kund off the road opposite the entrance to Tughlaqabad and drive for 200–300 yards, you can get a good view of the city walls looking back to the north-east from the dried-up lake bed. You can also get a good angle on Ghiyasuddin's tomb, but the walls prevent your seeing below the dome. Once in the precincts of the tomb, a wide angle lens emphasises the sloping walls and massive grandeur of the tomb very effectively, and a telephoto lens will enable you to get a good shot of the nesting parakeets. Early morning is probably the best time.

NIZAMUDDIN ** ♥

Although the early Mughal emperors (from Babur to Jahangir) were chiefly based in Agra, they recognized the importance of Delhi by making frequent ceremonial visits. These were begun just after the Battle of Panipat by Babur, who took formal possession of Delhi by calling at the important sites of the Qutb Minar area and Nizamuddin to underline the Mughal link with the earliest Muslim conqueror (temporal power) and the religious authority of the Sufi saints (spiritual power). These royal progressions round Delhi, always including the Nizamuddin dargah, were continued by Humayun, Akbar, Jahangir and Shahjahan. Shahjahan visited in 1634, 1635 and 1638, including Humayun's Tomb and his shikargah at Palam, but by his 1642 and 1645 visits he concentrated on Salimgarh and the site of his new capital and left out Nizamuddin's shrine (Koch, 'Delhi of the Mughals). The shrine is revered by Hindus and Muslims.

BIJAY MANDAL * ♥

JAHANPANAH * ♥

Having abandoned Tughlaqabad shortly after his father's death, Mohammed Tughlaq now set about fulfilling his master plan for the kingdom. Unlike his predecessors, however, *his* concept for the fourth city of Delhi was a protectively encircling *wall*, rather than a series of new buildings. Perhaps he got the idea from China? At first, his main aim was simply to consolidate, rather than to expand, his empire. There were still frequent border raids, the first of which he persuaded to withdraw on payment of a large ransom (according to Sleeman's account, this was possibly paid from funds supplied by his supporter Nizamuddin, who had just died). He therefore decided it was a priority to enclose Lal Kot, Siri and Tughlaqabad to form a new city, 'Jahanpanah', or 'Safe Haven of the World'. He did succeed in girding Lal Kot and Siri in a heavily fortified city wall, but ran out of money before he could include Tughlaqabad.

However, Mohammed Tughlaq realized that unless he expanded his empire he risked losing it altogether. He had annexed several territories in the Deccan: Kampili, the area where Vijaynagar was later built, Warangal and the northern part of the Hoysala kingdom, and this seemed to him a more central point from which to hold on to his by now considerable empire (Achar and Joshi). He gathered a large army and set about moving his capital to the Deccan at Deogiri (which he renamed Daulatabad), about 500 miles south. In 1338 he ordered the inhabitants of Delhi to move there in a body. A revolt at Multan soon brought him back, and the people were also allowed to return.

A new capital was begun, but famine struck and in 1345 Mohammed Tughlaq abandoned his scheme, allowing everyone to return to Delhi. Throughout his reign, rebellion was rife throughout the empire and, while seeking to put down an uprising in Sind in 1351, he was killed near Tatta, after ruling for some 26 years. Ferishta summed up his reign:

> he seems to have laboured, with no contemptible abilities, to be detested by God, and feared and abhorred by all men.

Spear describes Mohammed Tughlaq as 'cruel and changeable' but also 'brave' and 'very clever'. He was above all a great strategist and empire-builder, with a vision of a united community in an extensive kingdom. His move to Deogiri was not a mere capricious whim, as it is sometimes depicted, but a necessary part of his overall plan. The charitable description of him would be 'a broad-brush man' or a 'man of ideas'. He was not in any sense of the word, however, a democrat, and his attitude to the people (to paraphrase a later ruler in another country) was: 'When you've got them by the throat, their hearts and minds will follow'.

FIROZ SHAH KOTLA ** ♥♥♥

On Mohammed Tughlaq's death in 1351 his cousin Firoz Shah, the son of a Hindu princess, was elected to the throne by the army generals. After defeating the usual band of marauding Mongols, he established himself on the throne of Delhi before setting out on the by now equally customary campaigns to subdue Sind and Bengal (twice each). He recruited his army from the sons and relatives of those who had retired or died in service, as this helped ensure loyalty. On his return in 1354 he was able to settle down to what he really wanted to do: get everything in the empire sorted out and tidied up. He was a medieval version of a management guru or *Cold Comfort Farm's* Flora Poste. He instituted a revenue system and appointed officials to collect it. Dutifully concerned about Mohammed Tughlaq's place in heaven, Firoz Shah sought out the relatives of those who had been cruelly treated by him, gave them compensation in return for letters forgiving the wrongs done to them and put these in Mohammed Tughlaq's grave as testimonials to offer his Maker. He had it recorded in the *Wakf-Nama*:

> Among the gifts which God bestowed upon me, his humble servant, was a desire to erect public buildings. So I built many mosques and colleges and monasteries, that the learned and the devout might worship God in these edifices and aid the kind builder with their prayers . . . I was led to repair and rebuild the edifices and structures of former kings and ancient nobles which had fallen into decay with the passage of time, I giving the restoration of these buildings priority over my own building works . . . the expense of repairing . . . was provided from ancient endowments . . . [or, where there were none] I had villages assigned to them, the revenues of which would suffice for their expenditure in perpetuity (Elliot and Dowson).

The Conservation Society of Delhi regard Firoz Shah as their honorary founding president, and he was called 'The Father of the Irrigation Department' by the British because of the many gardens and canals that he built (Hearn).

Tughlaqabad had run out of water, Jahanpanah was a wall rather than a city — it was time to build another Delhi. According to an old proverb, three things were necessary: *Daria, Badal, Badshah* (loosely translated, River, Rainclouds and a Ruler). The ruler stood ready, the rainclouds could be hoped for, and of course the river was waiting in the shape of the Yamuna: Firoz Shah built the first of the *river-based* Delhis, the point being not only availability of water but also of transport and hence trade. Unlike the first four Delhis, only the inner citadel, the Kotla, seems to have been fortified: when Timur invaded, it was to Siri and Jahanpanah that the Delhi kings retreated. There was a tradition that underground passages connected the citadel to the Ridge, but Hearn regarded this as improbable, though:

> that one ran along the riverside through the palace is not so unlikely,
> but exploration would be extremely unpleasant, not to say dangerous,
> for the passage must be infested with snakes.

The visitor enters the Kotla from Bahadurshah Zafar Marg. The most striking feature is the tapering 14 metre high Asoka Pillar made of polished sandstone, which dates from the third century B.C. and was brought here from Topra in Ambala District by Firoz Shah in 1367. The locals told Firoz Shah that they called it 'Bhim's walking stick' (Bhim being the *Mahabharata* fighting hero after whom anything big and strong is often named), but by Bishop Heber's time in the 1820s the Asoka pillar had apparently become '*Firoz Shah's* walking stick' (Heber). A ball and crescent of gold were fitted to the top of the pillar, the inscriptions of which are still quite clear. They record Asoka's deeds in planting trees on all roads, digging wells at every mile, erecting *serais* for the benefit of travellers . . . all the deeds also claimed sixteen centuries later by Firoz Shah as evidence of *his* beneficent rule: apparently in what we demand of our rulers, the more things change the more they stay the same. Many mosques were built in Firoz Shah's reign: the Jama Masjid of Firozabad was much admired by Timur when he invaded in 1398, twenty years after it was built. He carried away with him a number of Firoz Shah's masons to build *his* great mosque at Samarkand. Although imitation may be the sincerest form of flattery, Timur's poaching the best craftsmen — not to mention his looting – put paid to much building in India for the next few years.

Firoz Shah died in 1388 and was buried on the edge of Hauz Khas, overlooking the tank that he had caused to be restored: not a bad monument to this great builder.

Note on Photography

As in all the other Delhis built on the Yamuna, the axis was basically east/west, so that the best time for photography is in the early evening. Care must be taken to avoid including the industrial chimney on the new bank of the Yamuna in the same photograph as the similarly-shaped Asoka's pillar – unless you are looking for the comical effect of deliberate juxtaposition!

Ugrasen Ki Baoli * ♥♥

In the heart of the 'ninth city of Delhi', i.e. the highrise business district, you suddenly enter this time warp and are transported back to the fourteenth/fifteenth century. Turn right (going north) at Kasturba Gandhi Marg onto Hailey Road and then left onto the narrow Hailey Lane, where you will see washing spread out to dry over walls

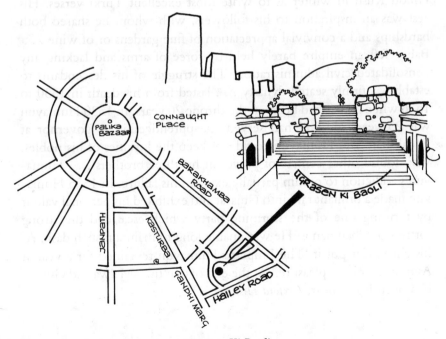

Ugrasen Ki Baoli

and on the ground. A little further on the right is the step well, and a moment of peace away from the bustle in what Y.D. Sharma calls 'one of the finest baolis in Delhi', possibly named after Raja Ugrasen, the forefather of the Aggarwal community. It is said that any Aggarwal new to an area could call on his fellow Aggarwals, each of whom would donate a brick and a small sum of rupees. With this seed corn, the newcomer could establish himself and be ready to help the next of his clan that came along in an enviable system of mutual help.

HAUZ KHAS * ♥♥

LODI GARDEN (TOMBS) ** ♥♥♥

An aside on Babur

The first Mughal, Babur, is usually left out of any account of Delhi because he chose to base himself at Agra instead, but the Indian Mughal empire was founded by him and it is worth reading Spear's description of Babur and the beginning of the Mughals in India:

> A very vigorous, artistic personality, as able to 'rough it' over the Hindu Kush in winter as to write most excellent Turki verses. His zest was an inspiration to his followers, with whom he shared both hardships and a convivial appreciation of fine gardens or of wine . . . Babur left an empire barely held by force of arms and lacking any consolidated civil administration. The struggle of his descendants to establish a firmly seated dynasty . . . lasted from his death in 1530 to 1576 when Akbar had been on the throne 20 years. In 1530 Humayun was 23 years old and had served an apprenticeship as governor at Badakshan. But Humayun could not keep the loyalties of his nobles, who found other centres of power in his three brothers . . . Humayun's addiction to opium partially explains his failure. In 1535 Humayun made a brilliant raid into Gujarat and exhibited his personal valour by forming one of the storming party which escaladed the strong fortress of Champaner. He was unable long to maintain such dash. As his chronicler put it 'The Emperor Humayun remained for a year at Agra and took his pleasure.' At the end of that time Malwa and Gujarat had been lost (Spear, *Oxford History*).

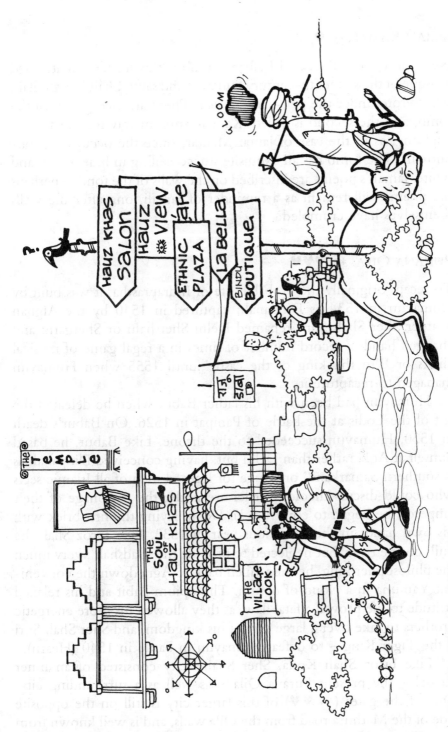

Hauz Khas 'Village' — Old and New

JAMALI-KAMALI * ♥

Near the Qutb Minar and Balban's tomb is this shrine and attached mosque of the sixteenth-century Sufi poet and saint, Shaikh Fazlu'llah, who wrote under the pen-name *Jamali*. There are two graves in the tomb, and the second is called 'Kamali' (presumably for the sake of euphony, as in the case of Jantar Mantar, since the occupant is unknown). The tomb has an exquisite stucco ceiling in blue, green and white. Jamali's poems are inscribed on the walls of the tomb – perhaps the poems will remain as a reminder of Jamali long after the walls themselves have crumbled?

PURANA QILA ** ♥♥♥

To recap: originally the probable site of Indraprastha, it was built by Humayun in 1534 as Dinpanah; captured in 1540 by the Afghan usurper Sher Shah Suri; renamed Delhi Shershahi or Shergarh; and changed hands a record number of times in a regal game of musical chairs or 'I'm the king of the castle' until 1555 when Humayun managed to recapture it.

Humayun had been with his father Babur when he defeated the last of the Lodis at the battle of Panipat in 1526. On Babur's death in 1530, Humayun succeeded to the throne. Like Babur, he based himself at Agra rather than Delhi but, having conceived Dinpanah as 'a southern Samarkand' or refuge for learned men of all Islamic sects who could discuss theology at leisure under the patronage of their emperor, he began to construct *his* Delhi, laying the first brick with his own hands in the auspicious year of 1533. Like Firoz Shah, he built on the river, but neglected to provide the 'Badshah': very much the philosopher king, he then sailed back to Agra down the convenient Yamuna in a cloud of opium. The opium habit and his relaxed attitude to life proved a fatal flaw, as they allowed his more energetic brothers to take over a large part of his kingdom, and Sher Shah Suri – the Tiger King – to defeat Humayun in battle in 1540 (Hearn).

Like Firoz Shah Kotla, Sher Shah's city consisted of an inner citadel – the present Purana Qila – as well as a surrounding city. One of the gates (** ♥♥) of this larger city is still on the opposite side of the Mathura road from the Qila walls, and is well known from the William Daniell engraving of it. Sher Shah spent little time in

Shergarh as he had the perennial problem of consolidating his strong-hold, and was killed in battle in Bengal in 1545. He was succeeded by his much weaker son, Salim, who reigned until his death in 1553 after which, for the next eighteen months, he was succeeded by no less than four warring would-be kings.

Humayun, meanwhile, had wandered through Sind, where he married the fourteen-year-old Hamida Begum who, while still in the desert, gave birth to the famous Akbar (whose name itself means 'great'). They reached Persia, where he was given asylum and military help by Shah Tahmasp in exchange for the Koh-i-Noor diamond, which Humayun had prudently taken the precaution of bringing with him from India, as an early form of American Express card. One can imagine the Shah pocketing it appreciatively, saying 'Yes, that'll do nicely'. There were in fact at least *two* diamonds with this name. Humayun's diamond had been presented to him by the family of the governor of Agra, in gratitude for his protection after the Battle of Panipat. It is not the same as Shahjahan's diamond, which was taken to Persia by Nadir Shah and, via Afghanistan and the Punjab, ended up in the British crown jewels and under lock and key in the Tower of London, from which nothing ever escapes (Howarth).

Humayun took advantage of the relative political instability in Delhi to 'strike back' on behalf of the Mughal Empire and regain his throne on 23 July 1555. But an army was not all that Humayun brought back to India from Persia: the two best court painters returned with him and founded the Mughal school of miniature painting. At first almost indistinguishable from the Persian school, these gradually developed a distinctively Indian quality until they reached perfection under Jahangir.

Humayun then settled down to putting some of his ideas on astrology and kingship into practice. He designed a wonderful astrological palace, with radiating halls of different colours, each with the name of a different planet. In each hall audience was to be given, on the correct days of the week, to the professions appropriate to each planet. One evening he was told that Venus ought to be visible and he decided that, if he could see it, it would be auspicious to announce the promotion of certain nobles. As Venus is 'the evening star' and would be the first star visible if stars could be seen at all, perhaps this was just a poetic way of describing a clear sky? Although Spear says that Humayun went up the Sher Mandal to enjoy the afternoon sun, it must have been the very *late* afternoon as, according to most sources, the stars were about to come out (over such trifles are battles of the pen lost and won!). Anyway, as he descended the steps, he heard the muezzin's call to prayer. He turned to kneel and, as he did so, slipped and tumbled to the bottom. On 24 January 1556, only seven months after regaining his throne, he died from his injuries. He has been called 'Humayun the hyphen', since his main achievement was to link the first Mughal inroads into India with their subsequent consolidation under his son Akbar.

As Akbar was in the Punjab, the fact of Humayun's death was concealed for seventeen days while a courtier dressed in the royal robes appeared at the daily audience until Akbar could reach Delhi. Even then, before he could ascend the throne, Akbar had to fight off Himu, the prime minister of one of the rulers of 1555, at a second battle of Panipat.

Note on Photography
The two main buildings are the octagonal Sher Mandal (which can be taken from any side) and the Qila-i-Kuhna Masjid, which you will want to take facing west to get the front facade, although the back, which visitors see first, has some interesting detail.

HUMAYUN'S TOMB *** ♥♥

Purana Qila's Humayun Darwaza looks back at Humayun's tomb, the awe-inspiring monument built to her beloved husband by his grieving widow, set in a Persian *'charbagh'* or square four-garden plan divided by stone water-courses, which had been introduced into India by Babur. The formality of the garden layout is not unlike André le Nôtre's Versailles, with the similar aim of establishing the grandeur of its patron. The style of this garden-tomb was to reach its zenith in the feminine perfection of the Taj Mahal, built as a widower's memorial to his beloved wife; Humayun's tomb is perhaps the Taj's masculine equivalent, both literally and to some extent architecturally, as the epitome of solid imperial style. For the tomb is immense: a newcomer to India could be forgiven for thinking that he was looking at a palace, not a place of burial.

Much thought has been given at every stage to the vista from that particular vantage point, and to developing a sense of expectation; the approach to the tomb is a long one, through three gardens and

The Plan of Humayun's Tomb

two archways. The tomb itself cannot be seen until the visitor reaches the last archway, when it is dramatically framed by the arch, but by a trick of perspective its *dome* is seen first as you approach the first archway, though it appears at that stage to sit on top of the second archway, and not the tomb itself. If you walk from the first to the second archway, watching the dome all the time as you do so, you will see it gradually disappear until it reappears, as if by magic, on top of Humayun's Tomb. (The dome of Rashtrapati Bhavan similarly disappears as you drive up Raj Path.)

We suggest that, to get an idea of the tomb's size and symmetry, you walk round the four sides first at garden level before climbing the steep steps to the platform terrace and looking at the tomb itself. You will see many openings in the tomb walls, some of which are blind alleys in an apparently confusing labyrinth, but if you look at a cross section of the tomb you will see that it has the elegant symmetry of a honeycomb as it echoes the 'hasht-behisht', or ninefold garden plan of the Mughals.

On your way out you should visit the adjoining Isa Khan's tomb (* ♥♥) and the serai (♥), if you are still feeling energetic.

Note on Photography

Again, the main facade of Humayun's Tomb faces west, and the gardens are better maintained on the western side, so the best time to photograph is in the early evening. The main gateways are also well worth photographing, as is the gateway to the serai, which faces north, and a second trip in the morning will allow you different angles and another chance to take in the tomb.

THE LAL QILA (RED FORT) *** ♥

'*The spider weaves its tapestry in the palace of the Caesars,*' said the famous Persian poet, Saadi, quoted by Heber in the 1820s to describe the decay of the once magnificent Shahjahanabad. Saadi was writing in the genre of Urdu/Persian poetry called *Shair-Ashoob*, lamenting the passing of greatness of cities, usually after a specific disaster. (This compares with the European tradition of 'Where are the snows of yesteryear?') The poet Ghalib mourned the 'death' of the soul of Delhi in the 1860s and Khwaja Altaf Husain 'Hali' wrote in 1874:

> O adventurer, your heart will be seared with pain and grief.
> Hearken to me, do not go into the ruins of Delhi.
> At every step, priceless pearls lie buried beneath the dust,
> No place in the world is so rich with hidden treasure.
> Even the traces of what reminded us of the city's destruction are gone,
> Dear heaven, can there be greater oblivion than that?
>
> (quoted in Gupta, *Delhi*)

So if today, as you wander through the gardens of the Lal Qila, you feel a twinge of melancholy as you try and imagine its former splendour amid the forlorn gardens of the present day, you are in good company and what you feel is not a new phenomenon. In truth, Shahjahan's city represented the height of Mughal achievement, both in power and artistry, and the city and the Mughal Empire both began their decline with the death of its creator, the 'Emperor of the World'.

Jahangir's son, Khurram, had fought his father in battle in order to take the throne in 1628, when he proclaimed himself Shahjahan, killing his potential rivals. (At this point, the student of Indian history feels entitled to complain about Mughal names, given their annoying habit of changing them once they become emperor. The British are no better – Kerr became Lord Lothian, Rufus-Isaacs became Lord Reading and so on!) Anyway, basing himself in Agra, Shahjahan began to build *his* city of Delhi, using the bricks of Firoz Shah Kotla to do so, and in 1648 he mounted the magnificent Peacock Throne, which had been seven years in the making. (It was he, of course, who built the Taj Mahal in memory of his beloved Mumtaz, and he was to spend the end of his life incarcerated in the Agra fort by his son Aurangzeb when he, in turn, deposed *his* father in 1658.) What is now the Ring Road was originally the Yamuna, and it is said that Delhi's inhabitants used to fish in it from the window openings of the fort until the latter half of the nineteenth century, when the Yamuna was so outraged by the events of 1857 that she picked up her skirts and flounced off to the east! Originally the only bridge across was the (temporary) bridge of boats, which can be seen in many of the old engravings. Let us imagine for a moment that we are seeing Shahjahanabad as the early travellers did and look at the court through the eyes of the French traveller, François Bernier. Writing in the mid-seventeenth century, he observed:

> Opposite the grand gate is a large and magnificent hall, decorated with several rows of pillars, which, as well as the ceiling, are all painted and overlaid with gold . . . In the centre of the wall that separates the hall from the *Seraglio*, and higher from the floor than a man can reach, is a wide and lofty opening, or large window, where the Monarch every day, about noon, sits upon his throne, with some of his sons at his right and left; while eunuchs standing about the royal person flap away the flies with peacocks' tails, agitate the air with large fans. . . . Immediately under the throne is an enclosure, surrounded by silver rails, in which are assembled the whole body of *Omrahs*, the Rajas and Ambassadors, all standing, their eyes bent downwards, and their hands crossed. . . . During the hour and a half or two hours that this ceremony continues, a certain number of the royal horses pass before the throne, that the King may see whether they are well used and in a proper condition. The elephants come next, their filthy hides having been well washed and painted as black as ink, with two large red streaks from the top of the head down to the trunk, where they meet. The elephants are covered with embroidered cloth; a couple of silver bells are suspended to the two ends of a massive silver chain placed over their back, and white cow-tails from Great Tibet, of large value, hang from the ears like immense whiskers. Two small elephants, superbly caparisoned, walk close to these colossal creatures, like slaves appointed to their service. . . . Other animals are next introduced;–

tame antelopes, kept for the purpose of fighting with each other; *Nilgaux*, or grey oxen, that appear to me to be a species of elk; rhinoceroses; large Bengalee buffaloes with prodigious horns which enable them to contend against lions and tigers; tame leopards or panthers, employed in hunting antelopes; some of the fine sporting dogs from *Usbec*, of every kind. . . . Whenever a word escapes the lips of the King, if at all to the purpose, however trifling may be its import, it is immediately caught by the surrounding throng; and the chief *Omrahs*, extending their arms towards heaven, as if to receive some benediction, exclaim 'Karamat, Karamat!' (wonderful! wonderful! He has spoken wonders!) Indeed there is no Mughal who does not know and does not glory in repeating this proverb in Persian verse:

'Agar Shah rozra goyad shab ast in
Bibiyad guft, binam mah u Parvin'

(If the monarch say that day is night,
Reply: 'The moon and stars shine bright')

SHAHJAHANABAD *** ♥ ♥

A walk round the streets and alleyways of Shahjahan's city can be combined with a visit to the Jama Masjid (*** ♥ ♥) and if pressed for time, the Lal Qila itself, but it is rewarding to spend a whole morning or afternoon just wandering at leisure without a fixed programme. Park near the main entrance to the Jama Masjid (avoiding Fridays because of the crowds) and walk 200–300 yards away from the Masjid, along the street at right angles to it, turn left into the maze of alleys and wander at random. Unless you have a very good sense of direction, you will soon have no idea which way you are going, but you can't get seriously lost, so just enjoy this different world – time travel without effort.

You could also take a bicycle rickshaw up and down Chandni Chowk, past the Town Hall where the clock tower, which collapsed in 1951, apparently never showed the right time because the pigeons persisted in using its hands as a perch (Gupta), and perhaps combine it with a visit on your way back south to the publishers and book distributors of Daryaganj's Asaf Ali Road, from whom you can buy books direct.

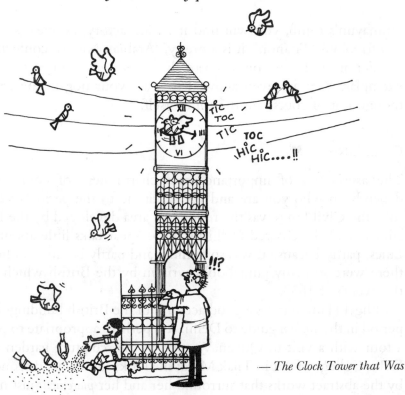

— *The Clock Tower that Was*

JANTAR MANTAR * ♥

This early observatory is a good place to combine with a morning's shopping in Janpath or the State Emporia of Baba Kharak Singh Marg. Jantar Mantar's present-day surroundings are one of the few examples where modern office buildings have actually enhanced a historical site. If you stand at the south side of Jantar Mantar and look north at its new background of Kuldip Singh's Palika Kendra with its outward-curving walls, Charles Correa's LIC Building and other interestingly shaped blocks, the effect is to alter the scale (like something out of *Alice in Wonderland*) so that the viewer sees them all as pieces in a jigsaw, a sculpture park or a Cubist painting. This serendipitous effect is surely accidental, not planned, but none the less magical on that account.

SAFDARJANG'S TOMB * ♥♥

It has been said that this is what Marie Antoinette's tomb would have looked like if she had lived in India. If you see it immediately after

Humayun's tomb, you will find it unsatisfactory, as Spear says. But as a frivolous 'Trianon', it is a pretty, 'Arabian Nights' confection to wander around – as compared to the severe grandeur of the earlier exemplar. You are even allowed to walk your dog in the gardens, though not of course on the tomb itself.

CIVIL LINES * ♥

The assessment of importance and charm here of course rather depends on who you are and your attitude to the period of British rule: the Civil Lines was the residential area developed by the British after Lord Lake entered Delhi in 1803. Spear talks little about Civil Lines, partly because it was so familiar and partly because, as he says, there were so many guidebooks written by the British which cover the events of 1857.

Nigel Hankin gives a good account of the British buildings of this period in the *Insight* guide to Delhi. It is perhaps appropriate to preface a tour with a visit to Queen Victoria in the sculpture garden of the Delhi College of Art in Tilak Marg; she looks somewhat disconcerted by the abstract works that surround her and her *placement* just next to

. . . . . an audience with Queen Victoria

a drainpipe, but she is at least not lonely, and on one of my visits I discovered a marigold in her hand. The same cannot really be said of the inhabitants of that 'sad and dismal plain' where the Coronation Memorial (* ♥) stands, the site of the 1911 Durbar, most easily reached by turning left at the signpost going north on the Outer Ring Road. Here stands the George V statue that was originally housed in the Raj Path canopy, surrounded by the houses of the greatest Princes in India to do him homage in durbar. He is now surrounded by the remains of Viceregal statues, some missing noses, and all more visited by pigeons than humans.

The tour can be completed with a visit to Flagstaff Tower (* ♥ ♥), a pleasant walk through gardens opposite the University, and the Mutiny Memorial (* ♥ ♥), built in the same style as Kensington Gardens' Albert Memorial. It is opposite the Hindu Rao Hospital on the Ridge, with a good view back over the city on a clear day.

New Delhi *** ♥ ♥ ♥

As Philip Davies says in his *Splendours of the Raj*, it is a curious fact of history that empires in decline often undergo a resurgence of cultural vigour before the end, and the British empire, like those of Spain, Rome or Austria-Hungary, was no exception. When, at the 1911 Delhi Durbar, King George V announced the decision to move the capital from Calcutta to Delhi, the assembled crowd was at first surprised and then overjoyed; they were less delighted in Calcutta.

The architectural committee of Lutyens, Brodie and Swinton eventually chose a site based on Raisina Hill, which they saw as an Indian Acropolis, with the Viceroy's house as the Parthenon. The British have always been fond of classical allusions: Herbert Baker, however, insisted on his Secretariat buildings *sharing* the hilltop with the Viceroy, citing the example of Persepolis as *his* classical justification. Sir Edwin Lutyens did not realize at the time the effect that this would have on the perspective of his Viceroy's House/Rashtrapati Bhavan (*** ♥ ♥) when seen from Kingsway/Rajpath – it all but disappears from view as you approach – and later fought a rearguard action to have the decision reversed. He was unsuccessful, and dolefully recognized he had 'met his *Bakerloo*' (Irving).

Hardinge's insistence that one principal avenue should lead in tribute from the 'Acropolis/Persepolis' to Purana Qila (the site of the first Delhi), and another to the Jama Masjid, was the inspiration for the equilateral and hexagonal plan (Mary Lutyens). This splendid perspective was later spoiled by Lady Willingdon who insisted on siting the National Stadium at the bottom end of Raj Path. Many stories about her circulated at the time; she seems to have been one of those battleaxes whose chief strength lies in a deep distrust of intellectuals and aesthetes, combined with an unshakeable belief in the superiority of her own judgement. Lutyens never forgave her for redecorating Rashtrapati Bhavan throughout in shades of her signature mauve (he called her a *'mauvais sujet'*).

Rashtrapati Bhavan, at 600′ long and 180′ wide, is built on a giant scale. It is bigger than any palace of the Indian Princes, presumably deliberately. It was designed above all to impress and, like other new buildings of New Delhi, to reaffirm the British intention to hold on to the Indian jewel in their crown for the foreseeable future. But Lutyens was no Albert Speer; unlike the architect of the Third Reich, Lutyens was not a man to use classical architecture on an awesome scale solely to buttress the authority of any ruler or raj. Although he took his New Delhi commission seriously, he had too much sense of fun to take *himself* entirely solemnly. At times it seems as if he were designing some vast opera set for an Indian version of '*The Mikado*'; he introduced stone elephants wherever possible and a row of lions on sentry duty outside Rashtrapati Bhavan – taken straight from the iron railings of London's Natural History museum. He borrowed the central dome from the Buddhist stupa at Sanchi, the red sandstone of the Mughals, and cream stone from Dholpur, Bharatpur and Agra. He invented a pillar design for the house incorporating stone bells, to recall the legend that the reigning dynasty would survive only so long as the bells of Delhi remained silent. Fountains played all round the house in the Mughal manner, and even on the roof: now turned off to save water, these saucers look like holders of the Olympic flame.

The city of New Delhi was built on a giant scale also: the broad sweeping avenues of Haussmann's Paris were meant to be strolled along by *boulevardiers*, but the two-mile long Rajpath was intended for processions, whether horse-drawn or horse-powered, and it is worth hiring an air-conditioned chauffeur-driven DTDC Ambassador to experience Lutyens' Delhi to the full. The rhythm of moving around relatively traffic-free New Delhi in this insulating glass bubble induces a mild hypnotic trance as avenue follows roundabout follows

The Filigree Gate of Rashtrapati Bhavan

avenue – slow, quick-quick, slow – and vistas of classical buildings succeed one another. Similarities to Caesar's imperial capital were entirely intentional: Lutyens called his creation the '*Rome of Hindostan*'. Most spectacular of these vistas is of course the long drive up Raj Path to Rashtrapati Bhavan – but almost as good is the road back, concentrating this time on the empty canopy framed by India Gate. Since George V was metaphorically relegated to the attic, there has been much discussion about who or what should replace him. Suggestions that Mahatma Gandhi deserved the honour have so far been rejected on the grounds that such a position would have been distasteful to Gandhiji himself, who would not have appreciated being treated as part of the panoply of the state. Those who wanted the canopy demolished have so far been held at bay by the argument that the very emptiness of the canopy is symbolic of the British retreat from India, and of course there is the purely aesthetic point that the canopy is an essential part of the Raj Path perspective.

There are other later architectural allusions to the British Raj in New Delhi: halfway down Raj Path are two post-Independence government buildings (Krishi Bhavan and Udyog Bhavan) whose surmounting domes look very much like *sola topis* – the classic pith

The Canopy without George V

helmet of the 'heaven-born' Indian Civil Service officer, a (presumably unconscious) allusion to the caricature of Lutyens with such a *topi* made out of one of his domes. And the Supreme Court (* ♥) in Tilak Marg is a PWD exercise in Lutyensesque style, which is one answer to the problem of how to add new buildings in the Lutyens zone without disrupting its harmony.

Lutyens designed staff quarters on the Viceregal estate and the National Archives (* ♥♥), as well as the buildings mentioned by Spear. He mocked Baker's bungalows as '*bungle-ohs*', and a rather warm house on Akbar Road became '*Baker's Oven*'. But most of the bungalows (and all official housing) were designed by Robert Tor Russell (1888–1972), the Consulting Architect to the Government of India from 1919 onwards. Russell also designed Connaught Place (** ♥♥), Teen Murti House (* ♥), and Queen's Way/Janpath (* ♥) including Eastern and Western Courts (* ♥♥); Arthur Shoosmith (1888–1974) designed St Martin's Garrison Church (** ♥♥); and Henry Medd (1892–1977) designed the Cathedral Church of the Redemption (** ♥♥) and the Church of the Sacred Heart (** ♥).

10,000 trees and 70 miles of hedges were laid out by W.R. Mustoe, an expert from Kew Gardens, who chose indigenous species that were sturdy, shade-giving and long-lived. Each of the major avenues had a separate botanical identity: tamarinds on Akbar Road, neems on Aurangzeb Road and arjun trees on Jan Path (Philip Davies).

Almost all survive, and the custom of planting trees on new roads has continued, these days usually sponsored by business houses.

The city was inaugurated in February 1931; only sixteen years later the British beat an (at the end almost hasty) retreat, and India became independent, with arguably the greatest British contribution to the country being the British-designed buildings.

DELHI SINCE 1942

Spear's cut-off point was dictated by the 1942 publication date and there could be little public building until after 1945 because of the war. Other preoccupations led to a hiatus until 1947, but then the ordered, garden-city layout of New Delhi received several shocks in quick succession. The first was the departure of the British – as the inscription about liberty around the gateway to North Block makes clear, the new city had not been built with the idea of leaving almost immediately. The government of independent India naturally wished to impose a new identity on their colonial inheritance as soon as possible and were in a mood to foster change. However, that change was not to be allowed to evolve at its own pace: Partition had meant the arrival in the capital of large numbers of refugees from the Punjab, Sind and Bengal who all had to be housed and find employment, foreign countries that had not previously been represented now wished to establish large embassies, business houses from other parts of India needed to set up a presence in the capital, and so on. The population multiplied overnight and a building boom reminiscent of gold-rush California was unleashed on the city.

Indian architecture had developed over thousands of years diverse styles of building which had one thing in common: they were all decorative and ornate – the absolute antithesis of Le Corbusier's '*machine for living*'. Unfortunately, when called upon to produce a great number of buildings in a short space of time, most of the architects of the 1950s and 1960s did not draw on this decorative heritage to create a distinctive twentieth-century Indian style. They were seduced by the Modern Movement and the joys of reinforced concrete to produce Delhi examples (that is, *in* Delhi but not *of* it) of every passing Western fad. Some of these buildings were good, even excellent, examples of their type (Yugoslav Embassy – 50s matchbox with applied 'sputnik' decoration, India International Centre – matchbox humanized by use of local stone and jalis, Polish Embassy – matchbox on stilts, Sri Ram Centre – matchbox on central pillar, STC building – matchbox spaceship, Khel Gaon Marg NCDC building – matchbox ziggurat, private houses – matchbox Moroccan, matchbox 3-D *Mondrian*, matchbox fortification . . .) but few make even passing reference to their Indian context. Percy Brown foresaw the problem:

> [with the introduction of concrete into India] there will be a tendency
> to subordinate individuality and nationality, so that all buildings will
> be of a standardised pattern.

Actually the standardized pattern, in retrospect, was one of the few merits of the style as it imposed a discipline and, repeated in street after street, a kind of harmony and unity (square, split-level concrete) through sheer repetition, although composed of individually unsightly elements imposed on us by the '*sado-modernists*' as they have been called.

Since then, a reaction against the sterility of these buildings has led to the pent-up imagination of our architects (given the richness of their heritage) being allowed full rein. Compared to America's zoning laws, for example, the planning regulations in Delhi exercise only the feeblest control over the built environment, which accordingly becomes good, bad or indifferent by chance. At its worst, '*In Xanadu did Kubla Khan . . .* ' becomes, shall we say '*In Malcha Marg did Mr Bahl, A Stately Pleasure Dome Decree . . .* ' as architect and client egg each other on in ever more lavish and bizarre constructions with decorative elements such as Venetian windows, composite pillars, *chhattris*, 'Hindu' corbelled as well as 'Islamic' pointed arches for window frames, Mediterranean balconies, etc. all applied to the basic matchbox in apparently random fashion as an afterthought. Vitruvius and the ancient *shilpis* would alike have been horrified at this misalliance of East and West.

More understandable perhaps are the honest attempts to copy a foreign style wholesale, such as the popular *Friends-Colony-Italianate*, modelled on the handsome Papal Nunciature in Chanakyapuri, or *Shanti-Niketan-Chateau*. The problem here is that the original was not designed for the Indian climate and, unaltered, lets in too much light and heat. The architect must either adapt the design by turning the eaves into full-scale *chajjas*, say, or affixing *jalis* or *jharokas*, thereby ruining the overall effect, or condemn his clients to sweltering summers. Faced with these two unattractive alternatives, the indifferent architect simply reproduces the basic unadorned concrete matchbox, as if the effort to adapt it to its environment were simply not worth making.

And yet there *have* also been architects throughout this period who have succeeded in drawing on the heritage of the past to create a style of building which is both contemporary and distinctively Indian. The first such was the Asoka Hotel (* ♥), built in red sandstone in the Mughal style (or plastered and painted in parts to look like sandstone). Buildings such as Sachdev & Eggleston's Modern School in Vasant Vihar (* ♥), C.P. Kukreja's JNU hostels (* ♥ ♥), Oscar Pereira's church in R.K. Puram (* ♥), Satish Gujral's seminal Belgian Embassy (** ♥ ♥), Raj Rewal's National Institute of Immunology

(** ♥♥), Upal Ghosh's Sanskriti Kendra, Anandgram (* ♥♥♥), and of course the marble lotus of the Baha'i Temple (*** ♥♥♥) are all examples. Here architects have reverted to the use of brick rather than concrete (warmer in winter and cooler in summer) whether painted, plastered or left unfinished; use sandstone facing with occasional marble, and prefer rounded shapes to rectangular (and incidentally Lutyens' 'rainbow arch'). These are all public buildings, but a walk round any South Delhi colony will also show private houses that demonstrate the growth at last of an Indian architectural vernacular that is also modern, which gives hope for the future. The effect is softer as buildings are built to blend with the landscape, increasingly treated as an important component in its own right. Lodi Garden has been re-landscaped, Nehru and Buddha Jayanti parks have added to Delhi's lung capacity, DDA and other new colonies *add* more greenery to the landscape than they *remove* in the course of development and Delhi is still one of the greenest cities on earth, despite the pressure for ever higher density housing.

So there are grounds for optimism but, and it is a big but, buildings need constant maintenance if we are to leave anything other than picturesque ruins for the generations that come after us. Rather eerily,

Some Modern Houses in Delhi

Lutyens' Delhi is showing the first seeds of decay — literally: for the last year peepul trees have been establishing a toe-hold all along the wall connecting the Secretariat to Vijay Chowk.

> The peepul is . . . apt to multiply in an erratic fashion, but its innocent vagaries do not take root in the soil, nor do they prey on their neighbours. They run riot, prodigal yet self-supporting, twisting and turning themselves like snakes in and out of the crevices of dead walls, beautifying what they destroy (Abbott).

Ghalib wept for the *soul* of Delhi; rather than weep for the — not unconnected — destruction of our capital's rich *architectural* heritage, let us be sure to preserve our beautiful buildings, whenever they were built, so that in the centuries to come our successors will still be able to share the pleasure that they give us.

— Sharing the Pleasure that They Give Us. . . . .

GLOSSARY

am	general or common (cf Diwan-i-Am)
amir	(pl. *umara*/'omrah') imperial official commander
anaga	nurse
auliya	saint
bagh	garden
baithak	reception room (*baithna* = to sit)
baksh	bestowing
baoli	step-well
baraka	divine power emanating from a saint's shrine
basti	small township
behisht/bihisht	heaven
bund	embankment
burj	tower or dome
chaat	spiced mixture of sliced fruit and vegetables
chahar-bagh/charbagh	garden divided into quadrants by water-channels
chandi	silver
chandni	moonlight
charpoy	simple wooden bed-frame, laced across with rope and string
chhajja	eaves
chhatta	roof or covered area, e.g. Chhatta Chowk = vaulted arcade
chhattri	domed pavilions supported by pillars
chishti	one of the four orders of Sufi (qv) mystics, brought to India by Muinuddin (d. 1236), whose shrine is in Ajmer
chowk	open area (square or octagonal) at an intersection of roads or markets
chunam	polished stucco made from powdered marble or shells,

common to many parts of India; was used extensively in Shahjahan's buildings

dargah	saint's shrine
daria	river
darwaza	gate or entrance
deccan	central and south Indian plateau (*dakhin* = south)
dharmsala	travellers' hostel, usually attached to a Hindu temple
diwan	hall; diwan-i-am was the hall of public audience, diwan-i-khas the hall of private audience
durbar	formal audience or court of a king
ganj	market place or suburb
garh	fort
ghari	a measure of time (24 minutes); a clock
ghat	landing place on riverbank or tank, usually with a flight of steps
ghazal	form of Urdu poetry, usually sung to a musical accompaniment
Gujars	north Indian community of herders, Hindu or Muslim, traditionally nomadic – numerous in villages near Delhi
gumbad	dome or tomb
haj	pilgrimage to Mecca
hammam	baths
hauz	tank or baths
haveli	mansion or ancestral home, implies some antiquity
hayat	life
hazrat	pious or saintly
Hindustan	today used as synonymous with 'India', earlier referred to north India, as distinct from the Deccan
idgah	open air mosque outside a city, where prayers are offered at Id
imam	Muslim priest
jagir	assignment of land; see also *mansab*

jahan	the world
jali	trellis or perforated stone screen
jamaat	congregation
jam'i masjid/ *Jama Masjid*	congregational mosque, not to be confused with *Juma* (Friday)
Jantar Mantar	corruption of Yantra Mantra; *yantra* – instrument, *mantra* – formulae
Jats	agricultural community of north India and Pakistan, including Hindus, Muslims and Sikhs – in the eighteenth century they became a strong military power, centred in Bharatpur
jharokha	window or balcony
jhil	shallow natural watercourse
kachcha	crude, unripe or unbaked (oppposite of *pukka*)
khan	lord or prince
khana	room or house
khanqah	saint's shrine or a hospice
khas	special or private
khwaja	honorific form of address for theological scholars
kos	a measure of distance, approximately 2 miles
kot	fort
kotla	small fort or citadel
kotwal	city magistrate in Indian towns before the British introduced municipalities and city police in the mid-nineteenth century
kushk	lodge or 'kiosk'
lakh	100,000
lal	red
madarsa	Islamic secondary school
mahal	palace or hall
majlis	a gathering
mandal	an area (can vary widely in the size implied)
mansab	official rank given by Mughal emperors, linked to military service, and paid in cash, or with a *jagir* (qv)

Marathas	caste name, but in the wider sense refers to Marathi speakers – Sivaji, a Maratha leader, carved out an independent kingdom in the seventeenth century which was extended in the eighteenth century by subordinate chiefs, including the Sindhias; the Maratha confederacy was defeated by the British in 1818
masjid	mosque; the plural is *masajid*
matka	earthen water pot
mela	fair
minar	free-standing tower or minaret
mo'alla	exalted
mohulla	neighbourhood
mumtaz	exalted (hence Taj Mahal)
mura	rustic stool or chair made from canes and string
mushaira	evening devoted to Urdu poetry recitation
nahar / nahr	canal
naqqar	drums (*naqqar-khana* is the name given to the approach to a palace where the drums are beaten at regular intervals)
naubat	keeping watch or beating drums at regular intervals
nazul	crown lands
paan	spiced betel-leaf
paisa, plural paise	small unit of money (at present, 1 paisa .01 of a rupee)
pal	measure of time (44 seconds)
pandit	learned man or honorific term used for a brahmin
phulwala	flower seller (*phul* being flower)
pir	saint
pirzada	son or descendant of a *pir*
pul	bridge
punkha	fan
purbia, poorbeeah	easterner, used for people of eastern Uttar Pradesh
purdah	curtain or veil
qila	fort

rais	men of rank
sair	walk or procession
serai	a rectangular enclosure with gates and niches for shops used as a traveller's inn
shah	ruler
sherbet	cool drink flavoured with fruit or essence, from the same root as the French word *sorbet*
shikar	hunt, hunting
shikargah	hunting lodge
shilpi	sculptor or builder
subah	province
sufi	Muslim mystics who belong to one of four orders; Nizamuddin Auliya belonged to the *Chishti* (qv) order
sukha, sukhi	dry
takht	podium, seat or throne
takhta	bier, i.e. ceremonial platform on which a coffin rests
urdu	military – the language Urdu originated as a lingua franca of soldiers in the Sultanate and Mughal armies
urs	anniversary celebrations at the tomb of a saint or ruler
vijay	victory
vipal	measure of time, a hundredth of a *pal*, i.e. 0.4 seconds
waqf	property endowed for a religious foundation
wazir	a minister – the origin of the 'Grand Vizier' of fairy tales
zenana	women's quarters in a house; men's quarters = *mardana*

CHRONOLOGY

Rulers	Monuments	People in Delhi . . .	. . . and Elsewhere
	Palaeolithic tools, Anangpur		Mohenjodaro, 2500 B.C.
			Greek civilization 800–323 B.C.
			Persepolis 518 B.C.
Asoka (MAURYA)	Pillars and rock inscription 3rd c. B.C.		Sanchi Stupa 3rd c. B.C. – 6th c. A.D.
SUNGAS	Earliest excavated site at Purana Qila site 2nd c. B.C.		
	Iron pillar at Qutb 5th c. A.D.		Roman roads and bridges
			St Sophia, Constantinople, 6th c. A.D.
TOMARS	Suraj Kund 10th c.		Masjid-i-Jami, Isfahan, 10th c.
Suraj Pal Tomar			
Anang Pal Tomar	Anangpur dam, 11th c.		
	Lal Kot		

152

Rulers	Monuments	People in Delhi . . .	. . . and Elsewhere
CHAUHANS			
Prithviraj Chauhan	Qila Rai Pithaura 12th c.		English and French cathedrals and universities 12th c. Angkor Wat 1152
IL-BARI TURKS 1206-90			
Qutbuddin	Quwwat-ul-Islam Masjid 1191		
Iltutmish	Qutb Minar 1st storey 1202 Qutb 2nd and 3rd storeys, Hauz Shamsi, Sultan Ghari, all 1231 Iltutmish's Tomb 1235	Qutbuddin Bakhtiyar Kaki d. 1235	Arhai Din ka Jhompra, Ajmer; Chittorgarh, 1200 Konark , Orissa; Padmanabhapuram, Kerala 13th c.
Razia Sultan	Razia's Tomb 1240		
Ghiyasuddin Balban	Balban's tomb		Carcassone, French walled city, 13th c.
KHILJIS 1290–1320	Canal to Delhi 1291	Nizamuddin Auliya 1253–1325	
Jalaluddin			

153

Alauddin	Alai Minar, Hauz Khas, Chor Minar all 1295 Siri 1303 Alai Darwaza 1310		
Khizr Khan Mubarak Khan TUGHLAQs 1320–93 Ghiyasuddin	Alauddin's tomb, 1315 Jama'at Khana Masjid 1316 Tughlaqabad 1320–24 Ghiyasuddin's tomb 1325	Amir Khusro d. 1325	Mohammed Tughlaq to Daulatabad 1327 Vijaynagar Empire 1336–1565
Mohammed	Nizamuddin's dargah 1325 Jahanpanah, Adilabad, Satpula all 1330s	Ibn Batuta in India Roshan Chiragh Delhi d. 1356	
Feroze Shah	Feroze Shah Kotla, repair of Qutb and Suraj Kund, Ridge and Malcha shikargahs, Hauz Khas madarsa, mosques of Begumpur, Khirki, Kalan, Kalan at Nizamuddin	Khan-e-Jahan Telingani, father and son, both 'prime ministers' Taimur invades 1398	China's Great Wall reinforced 14th c. Alhambra 1350

Rulers	Monuments	People in Delhi . . .	. . . and Elsewhere
SAYYIDS 1414–51	Shah Alam's tomb Wazirabad Khan-e-Jahan Telingani's tomb		Taimur's tomb, Samarkand 1405
Khizr Khan	Hauz Khas Idgah 1404		
Mubarak Shah	Mubarak Shah's tomb 1434		Inca Empire, Peru, 1438–1532
Mohammed Shah	Mohammed Shah's tomb 1444		Palazzo Pitti, Florence, 1440
Alauddin Alam Shah			Peking city planned, 15th c.
LODIS 1456–1526	Bare Khan, Chhote Khan tombs 1480s		
Bahlol	Bahlol Lodi's tomb 1489	Mallu Khan	Jahaz Mahal Palace, Mandu c. 1470
Sikander	Masjid Moth, Bara Gumbad and Shish Gumbad 1494	Mian Buhwa	Vasco da Gama in Calicut 1498
Ibrahim	Dariya Khan tomb, Nili Masjid 1505		

St Peter's, Rome 1506–1626

	Sikander Lodi's tomb 1517		
MUGHALS			
Babur	Jamali Kamali tomb and masjid 1528	Isa Khan	
Humayun	Dinpanah 1530s		
Sher Shah Sur	Imam-i-Zamin tomb 1540 Qila-e-Kuhna Masjid 1541, Shergarh 1541		Sher Shah 's tomb, Sasseram 1545
Salim Shah Sur	Salimgarh 1546		
Humayun again	Isa Khan's tomb 1547		
Akbar		Maham Anaga, Adham Khan Atgah Khan	Palaces of Datia and Orchha 16th c.
		Ferishta d. 1612	Agra Fort 1565–73
(MUGHALS AT AGRA 1556–1648)	Delhi Canal repaired 1561 Arab Serai Adham Khan's tomb 1562 Humayun's Tomb 1565–73 Atgah Khan's tomb, 1566		

154

Rulers	Monuments	People in Delhi . . .	. . . and Elsewhere
	Abdun Nabi masjid 1575		Fatehpur Sikri 1571–85
			Isfahan 1590s
Jahangir			Akbar tomb Sikandra 1613
			European Baroque 1620–60
			Jahangir tomb, Lahore 1627
Shahjahan	Chausath Khamba 1623		Taj Mahal 1632–53
	Abdur Rahim Khan-e-Khanan's tomb 1626		Fort St George 1639
	Delhi Canal extended 1638		
	Shahjahanabad inaugurated April 1648	Princesses Jahanara, Roshanara	Moti Masjid Agra 1640s
	Fatehpuri Masjid, Begum Bagh, Roshanara Bagh all 1650		Shalimar Gardens, Srinagar 1653
	Shalimar Bagh, Delhi		
	Jama Masjid 1656		
Aurangzeb	Moti Masjid 1659	Dara Shikoh killed 1659	

Bahadur Shah I	Ghaziuddin tomb and madarsa 1692 Zinat-ul-Masajid 1707 Sunehri Masjid (Chandni Chowk 1721)		Versailles 1669–1759 St Paul's London 1675–1720 St Petersburg 1721
Farrukhsiyar	Jantar Mantar 1724 Fakhrul-Masajid 1728		Jaipur 1720s
Mohammad Shah 'Rangila'		Battle of Karnal 1739, Delhi sacked by Nadir Shah	
Ahmad Shah	Sunehri Masjid (north of Faiz Bazaar) 1744 Qudsia Palace 1748 Sunehri Masjid (south of Lal Qila) 1751 Safdarjang's tomb 1753	Safdarjang Wazir 1748	Lucknow
Alamgir II	Najaf Khan's tomb 1782	Ahmad Shah Abdali invades, 1757 Madhav Rao Sindhia at Delhi court, 1785	Government House Calcutta 1799–1803
Shah Alam II		British victory, Patparganj 1803	Arc de Triomphe 1806
Akbar II	Begum Samru's house	Begum Samru	

Rulers	Monuments	People in Delhi . . .	. . . and Elsewhere
	Fraser's/Hindu Rao's house	Daulat Rao Sindhia	
	St James' Church 1836	James Skinner	
		Charles Metcalfe d. 1846	First railway line, Britain 1826
	Metcalfe House	Thomas Metcalfe d. 1853	
	Trevelyanganj	Bishop Heber in Delhi, 1820s	
		Emily Metcalfe (d. 1911)	
Bahadur Shah II		Zauq, Ghalib (d. 1869)	
The Revolt of 1857		Sayyid Ahmad Khan (d. 1898)	Great Exhibition and Crystal Palace, London 1851
		Zakaullah	
Delhi becomes part of Punjab province	Mutiny Memorial 1861		Albert Memorial, 1863
	Town Hall 1864		Haussmann rebuilds Paris 1860s
	Railway Station 1867		
	Lal Qila barracks 1860s		Victoria Terminus, Bombay 1887
			Eiffel Tower, Paris 1889

Coronation Durbar 1911–12			Taj Mahal Hotel, Bombay 1903
Delhi, a separate province			Gateway of India, Bombay 1911
Hardinge's State Entry, 1912			Canberra 1911–27
	Temporary capital in Civil Lines 1914–31		
	New Delhi planned and built 1914–31		
			Jodhpur palace 1929–44
			Term 'International Style' first used 1932
		Delhi Improvement Trust 1937	
India Independent			
PRIME MINISTERS			
J. L. Nehru 1947–64	Supreme Court 1955	School of Planning and Architecture 1955	Chandigarh (Corbusier) 1950s
		Delhi Development Authority 1957	Islamabad (Doxiadis) 1950s

Rulers	Monuments	People in Delhi . . .	. . . and Elsewhere
L. B. Shastri, G. L. Nanda 1964–65			Dhaka Secretariat (Kahn) 1960s
Indira Gandhi 1965–77	Nehru Memorial Library 1968–69; Sri Ram Centre, 1972		Sears Tower, Chicago, 1973
M. R. Desai, C. Singh 1977–79			
Indira Gandhi 1980–84	Asiad Village 1981–82; National Institute of Immunology 1983	Conservation Society of Delhi, 1982	Community Architecture Movement, Britain
Rajiv Gandhi 1984–89	Bahai Temple, Chhattarpur Temple	INTACH founded 1984	
V. P. Singh, C. Shekhar, 1989–91		TVB School of Habitat Studies 1990	
P. V. Narasimha Rao 1991–	British Council building 1992		

BIBLIOGRAPHICAL NOTE

All books referred to by Spear, Sykes and Gupta are listed here with their full title. Some other books of interest are also listed. All, with four exceptions, are in English. This is by no means an *exhaustive* list of books on Delhi.

VISUALS

Some of the earliest known 'views' of Delhi, by the Daniells, and others (including the Major Robert Smith who added the cupola to the Qutb Minar) are reproduced in *Mahajan*. Thomas Metcalfe's 'Delhie Book', illustrated by local artists, is reproduced by *M.M. Kaye*. Many travelogues of the nineteenth century are illustrated with sketches; one of the best is *Rousselet*. The 50 superb charcoal drawings by *Jhabwala* are a tribute to the city by an eminent architect. For photographs of Delhi, the best repositories are the India Office Library, London (Prints and Drawings sections) and the Photo-library of the ASI, Janpath, New Delhi. The text of *Yamamoto and Ara's* meticulous 3-volume photo-documentation of Delhi Sultanate architecture remains untranslated from the Japanese. For coffee-table decoration, *Brunel, K. Singh and R. Rai* and *Varma and Shankar* ('Mansions') are attractive.

MONUMENTS

Keay describes the excitement for British officers and civilians of seeing and dating Delhi buildings. The Delhi Archaeological Society in the 1840s enthused a young Indian, *Syed Ahmad Khan* (later famous as Sir Syed, the founder of Aligarh University) to write an exhaustive catalogue of Delhi's buildings. Though later writers – *Carr Stephen, Fanshawe, Hearn, Newell* and *Sharp* – borrowed much from his work, to date there is no translation of it in English. *Nath* has published a partial one where, he claims, 'Syed Ahmad's arrangement has been scientifically reclassified'. Serious investigations of the monuments can be found in the ASI *Report* of 1871, in their specialized *Memoirs* and in the booklets by *S.A.A. Naqvi* and *Gordon Sanderson* on the Lal Qila. Sanderson did much work on conservation, and wrote a good deal on Delhi monuments, but he was killed in World War I. (There is a commemorative inscription to him on the Qutb garden sundial.) The 4-volume Page/Zafar Hasan set of 1919 is indispensable; its Urdu equivalent is *Bashiruddin Ahmad. Y.D. Sharma's* official ASI Guide remains handy. We await the updated list of Delhi's monuments being prepared by the Indian National Trust (INTACH). *Ara, Welch and Crane,* and *Koch* ('Qutb' and 'Delhi of the Mughals') are prolific modern architectural historians. A lot of rich material on Delhi can also be found in general works of architectural history, such as the classic *Percy Brown,* and the recent *Asher* and *Koch.* The landscape setting of Mughal architecture is studied by *Crowe and Haywood,* and *Moynihan.* The articles in *Michell* are excellent, and half of his illustrative photographic plates of India are of Delhi. *Blake* is the only detailed account of Shahjahan's city. *Irving* remains the standard work on Lutyens' New Delhi, to be supplemented by *H.Y. Sharada Prasad. White* describes the work of Joseph Stein, who has designed many buildings in Delhi.

TRAVELOGUES

Travellers through the centuries have written on Delhi. Extracts can be found in *Kaul* and *Alexander* and, with some effort, in *Elliot and Dowson* and *Seir-ul-Mutaqerin. Ibn Batuta* and the Emperor *Babur* always make good reading, as do *Inayat Khan* and his French contemporary *Bernier. Dargah Quli Khan* likewise, though much is lost in the translation from his polished Persian. *Bishop Heber* is one of the liveliest of nineteenth-century observers. 1930s Delhi is well sketched by *Evans* and *Nirad C. Chaudhuri. Percival Spear* himself, with his wife *Margaret,* wrote an affectionate account of the Delhi they lived in. *Monk* is useful for information about Spear's college, St Stephen's.

HISTORY AND BIOGRAPHY

For the history of Delhi *Frykenberg's* collection has a number of good essays; this can be supplemented with *H.K. Naqvi. Beale* is a good *Who's Who* of Indian worthies. *Ferishta's* is a rare early work of history. *Digby* has fascinating insights into the art of warfare in the Sultanate, and *Morgan* has a lively account of the Mongols. Sultan Raziya has attracted two good biographers – *Jamila Brijbhushan* and *Rafiq Zakaria.* For the Lodis, read *Abdul Haleem. Rumer Godden* has written a pleasantly illustrated book based on the memoirs of Emperor Humayun's sister. *Francklin* is an interesting contemporary account of the early nineteenth century. *Spear* ('Twilight') and *Gupta* ('Delhi Between Two Empires') are accounts of nineteenth-century Delhi. *Banerji* has a biography of Begum Samru and *Humphrey Trevelyan* writes about his forebear, Charles. The 1857 Revolt has been written on extensively and we shall confine ourselves to recommending *Leasor*, *Llewellyn* and *Taylor*. *Metcalfe* translated the diaries of two Indians in 1857. The Civil Lines status-consciousness is analysed by *Anthony King*. *Embree* is an excellent work of reference. Sufi saints and the poets have remained largely the territory of Urdu readers, *Nizami* has recently published biographies of Nizamuddin Auliya and Roshan Chiragh Delhi, to be supplemented by *Troll* ('Muslim Shrines'). *Habib's* 'Khusro' is good, but out of print; *Mirza's* biography is an excellent substitute. Abdur Rahim Khan-e-Khanan has a biographer in *Debi Prasad*. Ghalib has been the most translated of the poets, and *Ralph Russell* and *Khurshid Alam* and *Pavan K. Varma* provide good biographies; the *Russell-Islam* team also have a book on three other earlier poets. *Akhtar Qambar* has an elegant translation of *Farhatullah Beg's* 'Dilli Ki Aakhri Mushaira'. *Christian Troll's* biography of Syed Ahmad Khan is very good, and *Andrews* on Zakaullah very moving. In June 1993 Delhi lost *Maheshwar Dayal*, who had an inexhaustible fund of knowledge about Delhi, which comes alive in the book listed; he wrote in Urdu and Hindi too.

FICTION

In the realm of fiction, *Ahmad Ali* is unrivalled for a sense of early twentieth century Delhi. *Hassan Shah*, 'India's first modern novel', gives a flavour of Awadh not long after Safdarjang's death. *Girish Karnad* has a powerful play on the controversial Sultan Mohammed Tughlaq. The Revolt of 1857 has again been a great draw, and writers from Flora Annie Steele (*On the Face of the Waters*) to M.M. Kaye (*Shadow of the Moon*) have written with varying degrees of authenticity. Two interesting exercises in delving into Delhi's past are *Khushwant Singh* ('Delhi') and *William Dalrymple*.

MAPS, TREES AND BIRDS

Maps of Delhi are available at the Survey of India office (above Bankura restaurant, Cottage Industries Emporium, Janpath); *Kohli* has produced a slightly dated Delhi A–Z. *Barton and Malone* is a unique guide-yourself-around-Shahjahanabad, and well worth buying. The Conservation Society of Delhi has published a set of maps of suggested walks in Mehrauli. Children and adults alike will enjoy *Khushwant Singh's* 'Nature Watch' and the action group *Kalpvriksh's* excellent books on the Ridge and on the Birds of Delhi. *Gupta* ('Our City') is aimed to help 8-year olds understand Delhi. *D. Vohra's* 'Delhi!'is good for dipping into. *Hobson Jobson* remains the standard work on Indian/English vocabulary, but *Hanklin* is a good attempt at an update.

ANNOTATED BIBLIOGRAPHY

G. F. Abbott, *Through India with the Prince*, London, 1906, quoted in Kaul (qv).

Elizabeth Achar and Girish Joshi, 'Tales Told in Stone', *The Pioneer*, 10 May 1992.

Bashiruddin Ahmad, *Waqayat-ul-Dar-ul Huqumat-e-Dehli*, 3 vols, Delhi, 1919 (in Urdu).

M. Alexander, *Delhi and Agra: A Travellers' Companion*, London, 1987.

Ahmad Ali, *Twilight in Delhi*, Delhi, 1940, reprinted, 1991.

Amir Khusrau, *Khazain-ul-Futuh*, translated by M. W. Mirza, Lahore, 1975.

C. F. Andrews, *Zakaullah of Delhi*, London, 1929.

Matsuo Ara, 'The Lodhi Rulers and the Construction of Tomb Buildings in Delhi', *Acta Asiatica* (Tokyo), 43, 1982.

Archaeological Survey of India (ASI), *Report for the Year 1871-72: Delhi*, reprinted, Varanasi, 1966.

———, G. R. Kaye, *The Astronomical Observatories of Jai Singh*, New Series, XL, Calcutta, 1918, reprinted, Delhi, 1985.

———, Zafar Hasan, *Mosque of Sheikh Abdun Nabi*, Memoir No. 9, Calcutta, 1921.

———, Zafar Hasan, *A Guide to Nizamuddin*, Memoir No. 10, Calcutta, 1922.

———, J. A. Page, *An Historical Memoir on the Qutb, Delhi*, Memoir No. 22, Calcutta, 1926.

Note: The ASI *Memoirs* Nos. 1–30 have been reprinted, Delhi, 1991.

———, J. A. Page, *Ferozeshah Kotla*, Memoir No. 52.

———, *A Guide to the Buildings and Gardens: Delhi Fort*, Delhi, 1937.

Catherine B. Asher, 'Architecture of Mughal India', *The New Cambridge History of India*, 1:4, Cambridge, 1992.

Zahiruddin Mohammad Babur Badshah, *Baburnama*, translated, reprinted, Delhi, 1970.

B. Banerji, *Begam Samru*, Calcutta, 1925, reprinted, Delhi, 1989.

Z. Barni, quoted in *The Empire of the Great Mogul* by Johannes de Laet, pp. 48–49, tr. by J. S. Hoyland and annotated by S. N. Banerjee, Bombay, 1928.

Gaynor Barton and Lorraine Malone, *Old Delhi: Ten Easy Walks*, Delhi, 1988.

T. W. Beale, *An Oriental Biographical Dictionary*, London, 1894, reprinted, Delhi, 1971.

F. Bernier, *Travels in the Mogul Empire 1656–68*, translated, reprinted, Delhi, 1968.

S. P. Blake, *Shahjahanabad: The Sovereign City in Mughal India 1639–1739*, Cambridge, 1991.

A. H. E. Boileau, *Miscellaneous Writings*, Calcutta, 1845.

M. Brand and G. D. Lowry, *Akbar's India*, New York, 1986 (Chapter 3 – The Kitabkhana: The Imperial Library).

P. Brown, *Indian Architecture (The Islamic Period)*, Bombay, 1942, reprinted, Bombay, 1956.

Jamila Brijbhushan, *Sultan Raziya*, Delhi, 1990.

F. Brunel, *Agra and Delhi*, translated, Delhi, n.d.

Cambridge History of Islam, Cambridge, 1970.

Nirad C. Chaudhuri, *Thy Hand Great Anarch! India: 1921–1952*, London, 1987.

H. H. Cole, *Architecture of Ancient Delhi: Especially the Buildings around the Kutb Minar*, London, 1872.

Conservation Society of Delhi, *Mehrauli Heritage Maps*, Delhi, 1993.

Sylvia Crowe and Sheila Haywood, *The Gardens of Mughal India: A History and a Guide*, London, 1972.

Canon Crowfoot, *Mission Life*, May 1872, quoted by Gupta, *Delhi between two Empires* (qv).

W. Dalrymple, *City of Djinns – A Year in Delhi*, London, 1993.

Dargah Quli Khan, *Muraqqa-e-Dehli: The Mughal Capital in Muhammad Shah's Time*, introduction and translation by Chander Shekher and S. M. Chenoy, Delhi, 1989.

P. Davies, *Splendours of the Raj*, London, 1987.

M. Dayal, *Rediscovering Delhi*, Delhi, 1975.

Debi Prasad, *Khan-i-Khanan Nama*, ed. M. H. A. Beg, Karachi, n.d. (in Urdu).

S. Digby, *War Horse and Elephant in the Delhi Sultanate*, Oxford, 1971.

H. M. Elliot and J. Dowson, *The History of India as Told by Its Historians*, 6 vols, reprinted, Allahabad, n.d.

A. Embree (ed.), *Encyclopaedia of Asian History*, New York, 1988.

H. Evans, *Looking Back on India*, London, 1988.

H. C. Fanshawe, *Delhi: Past and Present*, London, 1902, reprinted, Delhi, 1979. Lt. Norman's account of 1857 is on pp. 113–221.

J. Fergusson, *History of Indian and Eastern Architecture*, 2 vols, London, 1910, reprinted, Delhi, 1972.

M. K. Ferishta, *History of the Rise of the Muhammadan Power in India until A.D. 1612*, translated from Persian by J. Briggs, reprinted, Calcutta, 1966.

J. Finnemore, *Peeps at Great Cities – Delhi and the Durbar*, London, 1911.

W. Francklin, *History of the Reign of Shah Aulum*, London, 1794.

R. E. Frykenberg (ed.), *Delhi Through the Ages*, Delhi, 1986, paperback 1993.

B. Gascoigne, *The Great Moghuls*, London, 1971, paperback 1987.

Rumer Godden, *Gulbadan: Portrait of a Rose Princess at the Mughal Court*, New York, 1981.

J. & D. Goodall, *Delhi's History and Architecture – The Short Answer*, unpublished paper, 1990.

Narayani Gupta, *Delhi Between Two Empires, 1803–1931*, Delhi, 1981, 1986.

———, *Our City, Delhi*, Delhi, 1987.

M. Habib, *Hazrat Amir Khusrau of Delhi*, Delhi, 1927.

A. Haleem, *History of the Lodi Sultans of Delhi and Agra*, reprinted, Delhi, 1974.

N. Hankin, *Hanklin-Janklin*, Delhi, 1993.

———, 'The Northern Ridge', pp. 111–15, *Delhi/Jaipur/Agra: India's Golden Triangle* (Insight City Guide), Singapore, 1991.

G. Hearn, *Seven Cities of Delhi*, London, 1906, reprinted, Delhi, 1974.

R. R. Heber, *Narrative of a Journey through the Upper Provinces of India*, London, 1828.

Hobson Jobson: A Glossary of Colloquial Anglo-Indian Words and Phrases, 1903, reprinted, Delhi, 1979.

S. Howarth, *The Koh-i-noor Diamond: The History and the Legend*, London, 1980.

Ibn Batuta, *Travels in Asia and Africa*, tr. H. A. R. Gibb, London, 1929, reprinted, Delhi, 1992.

R. G. Irving, *Indian Summer: Lutyens, Baker and the Making of Imperial Delhi*, Yale, 1981.

C. S. H. Jhabwala, *Delhi: Stones and Streets*, Delhi, 1990.

M. C. Joshi, 'Some Nagari Inscriptions on the Qutb Minar' in *Medieval India: A Miscellany*, Aligarh, 1972.

Kalpvriksh, *The Delhi Ridge Forest*, Delhi.

——, *What is that Bird?*, Delhi.

G. Karnad, *Tughlaq*, Delhi, 1972.

H. K. Kaul (ed.), *Historic Delhi*, Delhi, 1985.

M. M. Kaye (ed.), *The Golden Calm: An English Lady's Life in Moghul Delhi*, Exeter, 1980.

J. Keay, *India Discovered*, London, 1981.

H. G. Keene, *Fall of the Moghul Empire*, London, 1876.

O. P. Kejariwal, *The Asiatic Society and the Discovery of India's Past*, Delhi, 1988.

Inayat Khan, *Shahjahannama*, trans. and ed. by W. E. Begley and Z. A. Desai, Delhi, 1990.

Sayyid Ahmad Khan, *Asar-us-Sanadid* (in Urdu; Delhi, 1846, revised 1854), reprinted in 3 vols, Delhi, 1991, edited by K. Anjum. This was translated into French by G. de Tassy as 'Description des Monuments de Delhi en 1852'. The only translation into English is a selective one by R. Nath (see below).

A. D. King, *Colonial Urban Development*, London, 1976.

Ebba Koch, *Shah Jahan and Orpheus*, Graz, Austria, 1988.

——, *Mughal Architecture: An Outline*, Munich, 1991.

——, 'The Copies of the Qutb Minar', *Iran*, London, XXIX, 1991.

——, 'The Delhi of the Mughals Prior to Shahjahanabad as Reflected in the Pattern of Imperial Visits' in A. J. Qaiser and S. P. Verma (eds), *Art and Culture* , Jaipur, 1993.

Narinder S. Kohli, *A to Z Road/Street Guide for Delhi*, Delhi, 1993.

J. Leasor, *Red Fort: An Account of the Siege of Delhi in 1857*, London, 1956.

A. Llewellyn, *Siege of Delhi*, London, 1977.

Mary Lutyens, *Edwin Lutyens*, London, 1980.

J. Mahajan, *The Raj Landscape: British Views of Indian Cities*, Delhi, 1988.

C. T. Metcalfe, *Two Native Narratives of the Mutiny in Delhi*, London, 1898.

G. Michell (ed.), *Architecture of the Islamic World*, London, 1978.

F. F. Monk, *History of St Stephen's College, Delhi*, Calcutta, 1935.

J. Morris, *Travels*, London, 1976.

—— & S. Winchester, *Stones of Empire*, Oxford, 1983.

Elizabeth Moynihan, *Paradise as a Garden*, New York, 1979.

Hamida K. Naqvi, *Urbanisation and Urban Centres under the Great Mughals*, Simla, 1971.

S. A. A. Naqvi, *Humayun's Tomb and Adjacent Buildings*, Calcutta, 1947.

R. Nath, *Monuments of Delhi: Historic Study*, Delhi, 1979.

H. A. Newell, *Three Days at Delhi (The Capital of India)*, Bombay, 1913, 1926.

K. A. Nizami, *Life and Times of Sheikh Nizamuddin Auliya*, Delhi, 1991.

———, *Life and Times of Sheikh Nasiruddin Chiragh-i-Delhi*, Delhi, 1991.

J. A. Page, *List of Mohammedan and Hindu Monuments: Delhi Province*, 4 vols, Calcutta, 1916–22. This is popularly called the 'Zafar Hasan Volumes' after the ASI official who did the survey.

S. L. Poole, *Medieval India under Muhammedan Rule*, London, 1907, reprinted, Delhi, 1980.

H. Y. Sharada Prasad, *Rashtrapati Bhavan – The Story of the President's House*, Delhi, 1993.

Punjab Government, *Gazetteer of Delhi District 1883–4*, reprinted, Gurgaon, 1988.

Akhtar Qamber, *The Last Mushaira of Delhi*, Delhi, 1979.

N. Qaiyum, 'Indo-Islamic Architecture's Death-defying Themes', *The Pioneer*, 1 September 1992.

F. F. Roberts, *41 Years in India*, 2 vols, London, 1897.

L. Rousselet, *India and its Native Princes*, revised and edited by Lt Col Buckle, London, 1875.

R. Russell and K. Islam (ed. and trans.), *Ghalib 1797–1869*, Vol. 1, *Life and Letters*, London, 1969.

———, *Three Mughal Poets: Mir, Sauda, Mir Hasan*, London, 1969.

Seir Mutaqherin, Survey of Recent Times, by Syed Ghulam Husain Khan Tabatabai, translated in 4 vols by M. Raymond, 1902, reprinted, Delhi, 1990.

Geeti Sen, *Paintings from the Akbar Nama*, Calcutta, 1984.

Hasan Shah, *The Nautch Girl*, translated by Qurratullain Hyder, Delhi, 1992.

Y. D. Sharma, *Delhi and Its Neighbourhood*, Delhi, 1964, revised edition 1990.

H. Sharp, *Delhi: Its Story and Buildings*, Oxford, 1921.

K. Singh, *Delhi: A Novel*, Delhi, 1989.

———, *Nature Watch*, Delhi, 1990.

——— and R. Rai, *Delhi: A Portrait*, Delhi, 1983.

W. H. Sleeman, *Rambles & Recollections of an Indian Official*, London, 1903.

P. Spear, *Delhi: A Historical Sketch*, Bombay, 1937 and 1945.

———, *Twilight of the Mughals*, Cambridge, 1951, reprinted, Delhi, 1990, under the title *A History of Delhi Under the Later Mughuls*.

——— and Margaret Spear, *India Remembered*, Delhi, 1981.

P. Spear (ed.), *The Oxford History of India*, New Delhi, 1958.

Carr Stephen, *The Archaeology and Monumental Remains of Delhi*, Calcutta, 1876, reprinted, Delhi, n.d.

K. R. N. Swamy and Meera Ravi (ed.), *Peacock Thrones of the World*, Bombay, 1993.

P. J. O. Taylor, *A Star Shall Fall*, Delhi, 1993.

E. J. Thompson, *Life of Lord Metcalfe*, London, 1937.

H. Trevelyan, *The India We Left*, London, 1972.

C. W. Troll, *Sayyid Ahmad Khan*, Delhi, 1978.

——— (ed.), *Muslim Shrines in India*, Delhi, 1989, 'Mysteries of Nizamuddin Dargah', pp. 112–24.

P. K. Varma, *Ghalib: The Man, The Times*, Delhi, 1989.

——— and S. Shankar, *Mansions at Dusk: The Havelis of Old Delhi*, Delhi, 1992.

D. Vohra, *Delhi!*, Delhi, 1993.

A. Welch and H. Crane, *The Tughluqs: Master-Builders of the Delhi Sultanate*, Muqarnas (Yale), 1, 1983.

S. White, *Building in the Garden: The Architecture of Joseph Allen Stein*, Delhi, 1993.

T. Yamamoto, Matsuo Ara and T. Tsukinowa, *Delhi: Architectural Remains of the Delhi Sultanate Period* (in Japanese), 3 vols, Tokyo, 1967–70.

R. Zakaria, *Razia, Queen of India*, Bombay, 1966.

INDEX

Delhi
1943

1 Shah Alam's Dargah
2 Delhi University
3 St. Stephen's College
4 Metcalfe House
5 Pīr Ghaïb
6 Hindu Rao House
7 Asoka Pillar on Ridge
8 Kashmir gate of city
9 Hindu College (old)
10 St. James Church.
11 Maidens Hotel
12 Cecil Hotel.
13 Salimgarh.
14 Chandni Chowk
15 Red Fort
16 Lahore gate of Fort.
17 Delhi gate of fort.
18 Jama Masjid
19 Shahjahanabad
20 Kalan Masjid
21 Zinat-ul-Masjid
22 Anglo Arabic college
23 Delhi gate of city
24 Firozabad
25 Lady Harding Medical College
26 Jantar Mantar
27 Viceroy's House
28 Purana Qila.
29 Sher Mandal.
30 Lodī Tombs
31 Tomb of Safdar Jung
32 Humayun's tomb
33 Mosque and tomb of Isa Khan.
34 Chausath Khamba
35 Tomb of Khan Khana

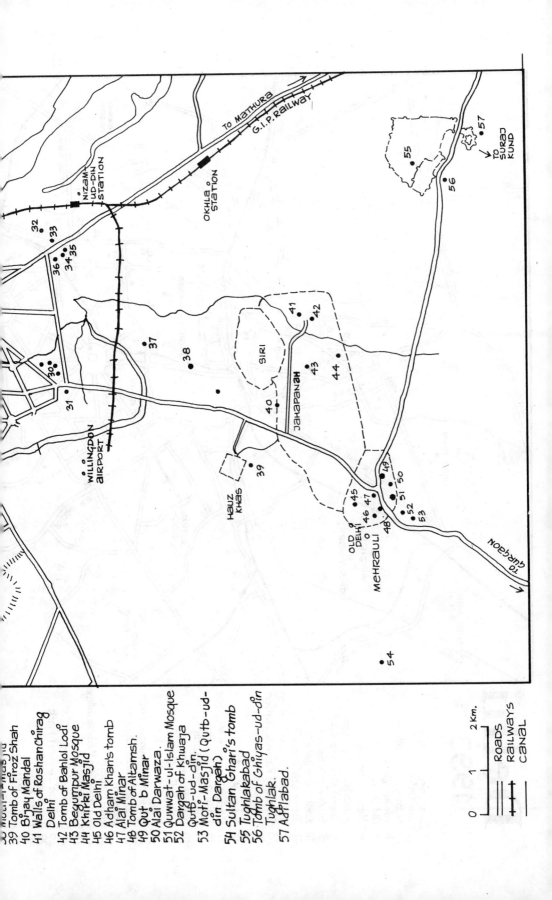

38 Moti-i-Masjid
39 Tomb of Firoz Shah
40 Bijay Mandal
41 Walls of Roshan Chirag Delhi
42 Tomb of Bahlol Lodi
43 Begumpur Mosque
44 Khirki Masjid
45 Old Delhi
46 Adham Khan's tomb
47 Alai Minar
48 Tomb of Altamsh.
49 Qutb Minar
50 Alai Darwaza.
51 Quwwat-ul-Islam Mosque
52 Dargah of Khwaja Qutb-ud-din.
53 Moti-Masjid (Qutb-ud-din Dargah)
54 Sultan Ghari's tomb
55 Tughlakabad
56 Tomb of Ghiyas-ud-din Tughlak.
57 Adilabad.

ROADS
RAILWAYS
CANAL

0   1   2 Km.

Delhi
1993

1 Coronation Memorial
2 Delhi University
3 St. Stephen's College
4 Hindu College.
5 Old Secretariat
6 Metcalfe House
7 Asoka Pillar at Ridge
8 Oberoi Maidens Hotel.
9 St. Xavier's School
10 Kashmere gate to city
11 Inter state Bus Trml.
12 New Delhi Railway Station
13 Old Delhi Railway Station
14 Chandni Chowk
15 Red fort
16 Jama Masjid
17 Raziya Begum's Mosque
18 Delhi gate of city
19 Firoz Shah kotla
20 Doll's Museum
21 Delhi Police Comm. office
   (opp. I.T.0)
22 School of Planning and Arch.
23 Indira Gandhi Indoor
   Stadium.
24 Birla Mandir
25 Lady Harding Medical College
26 Shivaji Stadium.
27 Connaught Place
28 Buddha Jayanti Park
29 Rashtrapati Bhavan
30 India Gate
31 Pragati Maidan

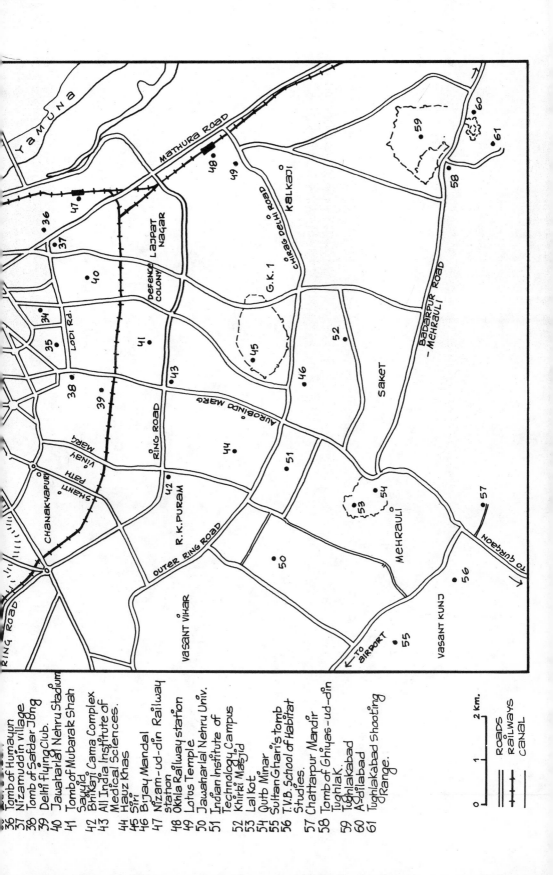

36 Tomb of Humayun
37 Nizamuddin village
38 Tomb of Safdar Jang
39 Delhi Flying Club.
40 Jawaharlal Nehru Stadium
41 Tomb of Mubarak Shah
   Sayyid
42 Bhikaji Cama Complex
43 All India Institute of
   Medical Sciences.
44 Hauz Khas
45 Siri
46 Bijay Mandal
47 Nizam-ud-din Railway
   station
48 Okhla Railway station
49 Lotus Temple
50 Jawaharlal Nehru Univ.
51 Indian Institute of
   Technology Campus
52 Khirki Masjid
53 Lal Kot
54 Qutb Minar
55 Sultan Ghari's tomb
56 T.V.B. School of Habitat
   Studies.
57 Chattarpur Mandir
58 Tomb of Ghiyas-ud-din
   Tughlak.
59 Tughlakabad
60 Adilabad
61 Tughlakabad Shooting
   Range.

0   1   2 km.

≡≡≡ ROADS
┼┼┼ RAILWAYS
─── CANAL